SRI SATHYA
Absolute Sole Lord

CW00616092

This work is a sensitive, intimate and transparent appraisal of Sai Baba—The Absolute Lord of Life and Death as only God can be. The sub-title of the book is the first line of a Hymn to Saint Teresa, a dedication by Richard Crashaw, the 17th century metaphysical poet. Saint Teresa was fired by the ember of divine love, while she was still a child of six and wanted to go to the Moors to embrace martyrdom for the love of Christ.

In this work also, the author expresses the supreme continence of affirmation, as he is touched by the terrors of death and learns, through experience, the lesson of a lifetime's death in love, ardour, selflessness and self-surrender. Written in the first voice and giving resonance to the true voice of feeling, it reads like a novel and is likely to have a universal appeal for all those who are seized with the passion of divine love.

Professor Krishna Nandan Sinha seemed destined to write this book as he was inspired in mysterious and inexplicable ways to put it together. With a doctorate in English literature from Arkansas University, USA, Professor Sinha formerly headed the English department at University of Bihar, Muzaffarpur and Sri Satya Sai Institute of Higher Learning at Prasanti Nilayam University in Andhra Pradesh.

Published by
Sterling Publishers Private Limited

SRI SATHYA SAI BABA
Absolute Sole Lord of Life and Death

Krishna Nandan Sinha

A Sterling Paperback

STERLING PAPERBACKS
An imprint of
Sterling Publishers (P) Ltd.
L-10, Green Park Extension, New Delhi-110016

Sri Sathya Sai Baba: Absolute Sole Lord of Life and Death
©1996, Krishna Nandan Sinha
ISBN 81 207 1564 0

Published by Sterling Publishers Pvt. Ltd., New Delhi-110016.
Lasertypeset by Vikas Compographics, New Delhi.
Printed at Saurabh Print-O-Pack, A-16, Sector 4, NOIDA
Cover design by N. Vashishta

For Malti Sinha and all those noble minds and beautiful souls, who, with anxious love inflamed, burn forever in the fire of divine love....

PREFACE

'Love, thou art absolute sole lord of life and death', is the first line of the famous poem, *Hymn to Saint Teresa,* written by Richard Crashaw, the seventeenth century metaphysical poet. The title of this volume has been derived from this line, as God is equated with Love. It seems to me that writing is something one does for love, and if love is of the highest kind, the love of the human soul for the Lord of the universe, the work in question takes on the beauty and splendour of genuine and intense heart-work, as it gives resonance to the ardours and aspirations of the heart and also to the unappeasable and peregrine apprehensions of the mind and the soul, and is richly suffused with images of poetry. *Sri Sathya Sai Baba: Absolute Sole Lord of Life and Death* may fairly be termed as a work of this nature. It is a work that I was destined to write.

The origin of the work dates back to 1973 when the Nessus shirt or the shirt of flame clung around me and I burnt in hellish fires and lived a tragic and tormented existence. It was at this calamitous moment that Sri Sathya Sai Baba came to live in our shrine and we worshipped him. Soon the first signs and emblems of his love and grace appeared in the form of *vibhuti* and *amrita* on his pictures. One morning as I stepped into the shrine to perform the *pooja,* I noticed a piece of paper placed in front of his picture. As I came closer, I observed a script scribbled in green ink on the paper. It read: 'You write a book on me.' I was mystified and dismayed and was at a loss to understand how the paper came to be there and who had written the message. I did not pay any serious attention to it, and forgot all about it. However, in the course of my reading of Sai literature I came across an anthology of essays by devotees relating their experiences. In one essay there was mention of the appearance of mysterious messages along with the reproduction of the facsimile of the script. Since the messages were in the *Devanagari* script, I compared the handwriting with the handwriting in the script which had appeared in our shrine. I was surprised to find a striking resemblance between the two. However, I felt that I was ill equipped to do the work, for my knowledge of the scriptures, the *Vedas* the *Upanishads,* Indian philosophy and religion was just peripheral. Besides, I did not know enough about Sri Sathya Sai Baba to venture to write about him.

So, I prayed to him: 'Baba, your message is a commandment to me, but I am perfectly ignorant and unaware of the august subject and my perceptions are tainted by the clouds of unknowing. How can I write about you? I pray to you to take me closer to yourself and show me glimpses of your glory and unravel to me the mystery and reality of your advent.' Having done this, I waited in stillness for further hints and indications. Fifteen years elapsed in living and partly living. In 1987, once again I was reminded of what I was likely to forget for all time. I suffered a stroke and was face to face with that fell sergeant, Death. It was then that Sri Sathya Sai Baba came to the hospital room at Prasanthi Nilayam as a saviour and I managed to survive. I felt the upsurge of spirit, as George Herbert felt after God's return:

> And now in age I bud again,
> After so many deaths I live and write
> I once more smell the dew and rain
> And relish versing.

> *The Flower,* 36-39

Looking into my eyes, he said affectionately, 'Professor Sinha, I am very happy with you. You will soon be all right, for you have still to do a lot of my work.'

Baba has solved many of my problems and has instilled faith and love in my heart and has set me firmly on the spiritual voyage. So, I have culled the blossoms of my love and devotion for the Supreme Lord of life and death to weave a coronet for him... in the fond hope that he will accept it. If the book pleases the discerning readers and induces them to the path of love and devotion, I shall consider that my effort has been rewarded.

Krishna Nandan Sinha

CONTENTS

CONTENTS

1
BE ABSOLUTE FOR DEATH

The eleventh day of January 1987 was a crucial and calamitous one for me, as it was on this day that I had my first ever date with Death, a virtual rendezvous with oblivion. If I came out of it fairly unscathed and unharmed, it may be termed as nothing short of a miracle. But miracles do happen when you are living at a celestial place, so close to the zone of light. So, on that fateful morning at Prasanthi Nilayam I had my intimations with immortality and saw, as though in a flashing of the shield, the burning bush. Thus, the encounter with Death, oblivion and near certain dissolution turned out to be climactic and salutary, a consummation devoutly to be wished for.

Had I been a poet, I would have composed a hymn in praise of the glory of the Lord, a requiem for the expression of my gratitude to the divine. But at that time my senses were too dazed and confused to order and discipline the dissolving squads of emotion to enable me to find apt metaphors for poetry. Surely at that crucial time when I had the quintessential awareness of divine grace and protective love, I seemed to have missed the meaning. But now when I view the experience in retrospect with the additional advantage of hindsight I feel that an approach to the experience has restored the meaning, though in a different form. It may not be far from the truth to affirm that during these crucial moments when I stood perilously at the frontier of life and death and lay suspended between time and timelessness, the state of my mind might have been the same as that of Richard Crashaw, the seventeenth century metaphysical poet, who, in his famous poem *A Hymn to St. Teresa* gave resonance to his

innermost feeling for the Supreme Being: 'Love, thou art
Absolute sole lord of life and death.' And Love, in my case, was
none other than Sri Sathya Sai Baba, the divine made human,
the incarnation of the supreme Krishna and Jesus Christ come
again.

It may be necessary at the very outset to relate the
contours of my experience in all its texture and detail, as I
write my intimate journal on these spindrift pages. Like many
blessed souls I was living at Prasanthi Nilayam, the abode of
peace. After my superannuation as Professor and Head of the
English Department, Bihar University, I was one of the few
fortunate ones who were asked to serve at the feet of the Lord.
I was offered the most prestigious assignment as Professor and
Chairman of the English Faculty at Sri Sathya Sai Institute of
Higher Learning, a deemed university founded by Sri Sathya
Sai Baba. I landed at Prasanthi Nilayam in July, 1985 and
took up my new assignment. It was indeed the most exciting
and challenging assignment of my life. I had spent almost a
lifetime in the constant pursuit of my calling, the noble
profession of teaching at different universities in Northern
India and had also spent a couple of years at an American
university, but never before had I experienced the thrill of
total involvement with my work and the unique satisfaction of
working for an ideal. The educational programme of the
university shaped by the Lord Himself and implemented by
Professor Vinayak Krishna Gokak, the founder Vice-
Chancellor of the Institute, seemed to me to be flawless and I
soon discovered that work here was prayer involving duty,
discipline, and devotion. The academic curriculum, the courses
of study, the standard of research... all were of the highest
order. The Institute was an elite institution rated highly by the
Government of India and by the people. The teachers and
students were bound together by the common link that they
were all ardent devotees of Sri Sathya Sai Baba. I felt
radiantly happy to be given the opportunity to serve here and
to become an instrument for the service of the Lord. I felt
blessed and everything about me was blessed. However, I must
confess that in spite of tremendous suffering and travails in
my life, I had not yet reached the still centre and had still to go
a long way on the path of attaining spiritual discipline and

sadhana and perhaps that was why God had ordained suffering for me and baptized me in more pain than I could bear. Perhaps, my *karma* had not yet completely burnt out, and perhaps I was not yet ready to receive the illumination that comes to one who surrenders completely to the divine. Ardour, selflessness and self-surrender are verily the key to love, both human and divine. I was of human love possessed and had not crossed my conscious and the sullen 'I'. I still nursed my ego, and prided myself in the prowess of my intellect. Perhaps this pervasive nature of self-love was the destructive element which had destroyed the foundation and fabric of faith.

I needed some kind of jolt to remind me what I was likely to forget: the essence of human aspiration, man's destiny and destination, his ultimate merger with the divine. For this, it was necessary to shed the ego, to cross the 'I' and practise detachment from self, from things and from persons. Such a condition is difficult to achieve, for the limits of human aspirations and the sway of unageing intellect are hurdles. That may be the reason why even the greatest saints, mystics and seers had to go through the crucible of unmerited suffering before they could have their epiphany and vision, and hold communion with God. It is common knowledge that some of the greatest religious poets have had their precious and unique apprehensions after having gone through the mill of suffering in their personal *inferno* and the chastening flame of purgation. Dante had the vision of the Supreme Reality in the empyrean when he saw Love in the image of light. 'Within its depth I saw, bound by love in one volume, the scattered leaves of all the universe, substance and accidents and their relations, as though together fused after such fashion that what I tell of is one single flame.'

And George Herbert also faced the calamitous experience of physical and mental affliction before faith broke into his life:

My flesh began unto my soul in pain,
Sickness cleave my bones;
Consuming agues dwell in every vein,
And tune my breath to groans,
Sorrow was all my soul; I scarce believed,
Till grief did tell me roundly, that I lived.

Affliction, 25-30

After a night of disturbed sleep when I woke up at dawn, it was dark in the morning. I looked out through the window at the azure sky and heard the soft and insistent rustle of leaves and the faint echo of voices on the street. At Prasanthi Nilayam, normally the activities of life—action, contemplation and devotion—start pretty early even before sunrise and daybreak. The faint echo of *bhajans,* chanted by the devotees in the premises of the *ashram* floated up in the air, and it was a reminder to me, if any reminder was needed, that the time to get up for yet another day of work and worship had begun. However, I was not feeling fresh or buoyant as usual. The long hours of waking during the night which had appeared to be interminable, made me feel uneasy and unstable. But, by force of habit, I prepared myself for a hurried walk down the street to the *ashram* to fetch milk. I had a special reason to hurry up as the annual sports of the Institute was slated for that day and my presence there was necessary. As I walked down the street, I noticed milkmaids from the nearby villages clustering at the gate of the temple to carry out their business. But I went straight to the milk booth inside the *ashram* where pure milk from *Gokulam,* the dairy, was available. My head was unusually heavy and my steps faltered. I did not know why. Maybe, the loss of sleep in the night before accounted for this heaviness. As I moved towards the teachers' quarters with the milk container, I noticed that the shops were open and eating places were unusually crowded. I noticed that the crowd of people flowed across the street towards the Hill View Stadium, the venue of the annual sports. Everyone wanted to reach there and occupy the first row or the vantage point from where he could see the face of Sri Sathya Sai Baba who, as the Chancellor of the university, was to inaugurate the function. I rushed back to my apartment to find that stillness pervaded there. My wife and daughter were in the kitchen, busy with their domestic chores. I handed over the milk container to my wife and asked her to prepare tea.

'I am not feeling quite well. I did not sleep too well last night and so there is heaviness in the head,' I said casually.

'You are working hard these days and do not take a proper rest. I have been reminding you time and again to go to hospital to get your blood pressure checked up, but you do not seem to care,' my wife said with concern.

'I'll get my blood pressure checked the first thing tomorrow. Today, attendance at the sports meet will keep me engaged. You know, the teachers also have to participate in some items. You remember last year we enjoyed the whole thing and Swami smiled as he watched us,' I muttered and moved to the bedroom to change my clothes.

'Do you want your breakfast now or would rather take it later after the sports are over?' my wife queried.

'I am not particularly keen on having breakfast. I suppose you will be also going to the stadium. We might skip breakfast this morning. Some tea is all I need at the moment,' I said.

As I sipped the cup of steaming hot tea I noticed the first rays of the sun falling on the window pane. The voice of a bird of ill-omen, flying in the sky at this very early hour of the dawn, reverberated in the air. It was not a soft, melodious note like that of the birds of spring. It did not remind me of the insistent and compelling call of life, either of the cuckoo or of the nightingale. Nor did it represent the summons of the humming bird which I often used to hear while I was in America, the sound that fascinated me endlessly and I allowed the temptation to go on by and pursue the right course of duty and discipline. But the strange and inexplicable, even discordant note of the bird flying high in the sky, warbling a sinister note at the hour of the dawn seemed to me to be the harbinger of death and dissolution. However, I brushed aside such a gloomy thought on a morning like this, specially at this celestial place, hallowed by the presence of the Lord. I walked out of my apartment and joined the row of devotees marching gaily on the road leading to the Hill View Stadium. Soon I reached the College of Arts and Sciences where the department of English was located. I realised just then that the day before I had written a few urgent letters which I had placed in the drawer in my office. I wanted to get those letters and post them so that these could go with the morning mail. I opened the lock of the room and picked up the letters. I looked at the electronic clock on the wall. It was thirty minutes past seven and I still had half an hour at my disposal as the inauguration of the sports was slated to be held at 8 a.m. My head was reeling like a top and inwardly I felt nervous. 'What is happening to me...?' I wondered. It was nothing new—I had

not had a restful sleep in the night and faced the inner weather
of incessant tensions. But I had come out of it all fresh and
radiant like lilacs in the spring. But this morning it seemed to
be different. The artery and veins on the right and left temple
throbbed and langour held its sway over my body. I went to the
attached lavatory intending to sprinkle some cold water on the
head and wash my face and eyes. I bolted the door from inside,
opened the tap and washed my face and eyes with a handful of
water. It was then that a wave-like surge of blood rushed
upward towards my head and I staggered, unable to keep my
balance. I slumped on the floor in a heap. I realised that I was
not in a swoon and my mind was still working fast. With the
intention of self-preservation I tried my level best to gather
myself and stand up. But it was by no means easy. My left limb
had grown numb as though all the energy had been drained
out. The heaviness in the head increased further. A film of
mist floated before my eyes. A fitful fever seemed to sing in my
mental wires, but my perceptions were not yet hazy.
Awareness dawned upon me that I had probably suffered a
stroke and I was in a state of utter and unprecedented fright.
It was truly a crisis, the likes of which I had never before
experienced. While I knew that the human condition was
perilous and the prospect of death and disaster always loomed
large over the horizon to remind mankind how vulnerable and
transient life is, I had never imagined how terrifying,
frightening and painful such an experience could be. With all
these thoughts uppermost in my reeling brain, I made a great
effort to calm myself and think of the best way to extricate
myself from this difficult and critical situation. But my left
limb refused to obey the call of my brain and did not stir at all.
All sense of movement was gone and there was nothing I could
do about it. Panic gripped my mind and I believed that I had no
option but to die within the roomless confines of a lavatory.
The day being Sunday, there was little chance that anyone
would come to the Department and it would not be before the
forenoon of Monday that someone would stumble over my body
and tell the world what had happened. Gripped by an
overwhelming sense of fright and panic and thinking of those
who would die after me, I took recourse to the one and only
choice available to all those who find themselves in a

whirlpool, face to face with the danger, despair, defeat and
annihilation... prayer. The handsome and sacred figure of
Swami with the sunshiny face and crescent of hair, like those
of Lord Siva, flashed in my mind. 'Swami, I do not want to die
in this fashion. I have still miles to go and many promises to
keep before I sleep. Do please save me and pull me out of this
sea of misery. Please, redeem me, Swami. I had come all the
way to Prasanthi Nilayam with the sole intention of serving
you. If I cease to be what shall my people do? I am not yet ready
for death or for the mystical transcendence to find life in death.
I pray to you with all the intensity at my command. Send some
assistance...' I prayed most fervently even while my conscious
mind was in an eclipse. Unable to withstand the stress and the
strain and caught up in a phase of complete inertia and
physical incapacity, I reclined my head on the floor. I do not
remember how long I remained in this state. But once again
my conscious mind asserted itself and I chanted my prayer to
Swami with renewed vigour. I visualised mentally the vast
congregation of people standing in a circle, listening to the
discourse of Sri Sathya Sai Baba. I also visualised the Faculty
members occupying the centre stage, looking like
constellations around Swami. And I wondered if anyone
missed me there. Who, except Swami, would know my plight?
Then I thought of my wife and daughter who might be
witnessing the sports show little knowing that I was
desperately in need of help. The thought of my family and my
deep emotional attachment to them gave me an additional
impetus to devise ways and means to move out of the prison
house that was the lavatory, stuffy and sunless. I exercised my
right limb which, fortunately, worked as strongly as before
and managed to sit up. Leaning on the right hand and leg and
dragging the left leg, I crawled slowly towards the door and,
balancing my body somehow, I opened the door latch. The
momentum of the action was such that I fell on the left side.
But the door was ajar now. I surmised that I would need to
crawl several yards dragging myself if I were to reach the
entrance of my Department. I shuddered to think of the
distance and the quantum of energy involved in the exercise,
but there was no time to pause or relax. The effort had to be
made at all costs. If I could get out of the office, I would be on

the verandah and the chances were very strong that someone coming to the front gate of the college could spot me and lend a helping hand and bring relief. So it was a question of life and death and I decided to make the effort in spite of the general weakness and mounting fatigue. It took me nearly an hour and a half to traverse that distance of five yards. I slumped on the floor several times and got temporary respite from the strenuous effort. I finally found myself near the door to the entrance. As the door was already open, I crossed the threshold and found myself in the verandah from where I had a view of the beautiful lawn adorned with gay flowers. The clamour of the street was faintly audible as the business of life went on as usual. It was a fateful journey for me, from the lavatory to the verandah, the interior to the exterior, from death to life, as it were! My mind, however, kept on journeying, on the symbolic plane. It was not like Dante's divine pilgrimage from the *Inferno* to *Paradiso*. Nor did it echo or reiterate Eliot's resolve, embodied in the lines: 'We shall never cease from exploration.' It was, if anything, a temporary stay against confusion, a stopping by the wood on a dismal morning when the straight way was lost and there were many menacing monsters, threatening annihilation. And like Robert Frost, I felt:

> The woods are lovely, dark and deep
> But I have promises to keep,
> And miles to go before I sleep
> And miles to go before I sleep.
> *Stopping by the Woods on a Snowy Evening*

However, what those promises were, I myself did not know. My first impulse was that of survival. I looked longingly at the row of flowers swaying their heads gently in the breeze and cast an eager glance at the main entrance of the college in the hope that somebody would unexpectedly turn up to render help to me. I waited and waited, feverishly suspended between sleep and waking, agonising moments of consciousness and the fitful duration of dizziness and oblivion, in fact, alternating between life and death. The haunting melody of some musical bird came from across the hills. The musical note was a distinctive one, not like the one I had heard early in the morning from the throat of the bird of ill omen. This note, on the contrary was of the essence of life... life-embracing and redemptive. It was indeed the voice of some immortal bird meant to resurrect me from the dark valleys of death and oblivion back to life and my feeling was akin to what John Keats expressed beautifully in the *Ode to a Nightingale:*

> Darkling I listen; and, for many a time
> I have been half in love with easeful Death
> Call'd him soft names in many a mused rhyme,
> To take into the air my quiet breath;
> Now more than ever seems it rich to die,
> To cease upon the midnight with no pain,
> While thou art pouring forth thy soul abroad
> In such an ecstasy—.
> Still wouldst thou sing, and I have ears in vain—
> To thy high requiem become a sod.
>
> *Ode to a Nightingale,* Stanza vi

The alternating movement from life to death, the mutual thrust and recoil and their rich co-existence seemed very real to me at the moment. During that moment of the intensest and clearest perception of Death I thought time and again of the greatest death poetry which I had read. Claudio's frenzied lust for life and fear of Death has been voiced powerfully in Shakespeare's *Measure for Measure:*

> Ay, but to die, and go we know not where
> To lie in cold obstruction, and to rot;
> This sensible warm motion to become
> A kneaded clod; and the delighted spirit
> To bathe in fiery floods or to reside
> In thrilling regions of thick-ribbed ice;
> To be imprison'd in the viewless winds,
> And blown with restless violence round about
> The pendent world; or to be worse than worst
> Of those that lawless and incertain thought
> Imagine howling—'tis too horrible.
> The weariest and most loathed worldly life
> That age, ache, penury, and imprisonment,

Can lay on nature is a paradise
To what we fear of death.
Measure for Measure, 3.i. 119-133

And the Duke's injunction to Claudio, which is equally
great poetry, amounts to a wholesale rejection of life:

Be absolute for death, either death or life
Shall thereby be sweeter. Reason thus with life,
If I do lose thee, I do lose a thing
That none but fools would keep. A breath thou art,
Servile to all the skyey influences,
That do this habitation where thou keep'st
Hourly afflict. Merely, thou art Death's fool;
For him thou labours't by thy flight to shun
And yet thou runs't toward him still. Thou art not noble;
For all th' accommodations that thou bears't
Are nurs'd by baseness. Thou art by no means valiant;
For thou dost fear the soft and tender fork
Of a poor worm. Thy best of rest is sleep,
And that thou oft provoks't; yet grossly fears't
Thy death which is no more....
Thou hast nor youth nor age.—
But, as it were, an after-dinner' sleep,
Dreaming on both.
Measure for Measure, 3.i. 5-33

I recall vividly how during those critical moments my mind
ranged countries and promenades and my imagination
resurrected the images of poetry so dear to me. I also
remembered some lines written by a famous poet, which
negated the horrors of death and glorified it as a
consummation to be devoutly wished for. The suffering of the
body and mortification of the flesh were desirable inasmuch as
they hastened the process of spiritual ascent. The loss to the
body meant gain to the soul. Shakespeare, in one of his
sonnets, has said as much. And **Wallace** Stevens in *Sunday
Morning* speaks of death as the **mother** of beauty. However,
my aversion to death and shying **away** from it was entirely
human because I had not yet seen the burning bush and was
not yet free from cravings. And as I have said earlier, I was not
yet ready for death.

I waited for hours without end, lying on the floor in a supine posture. I kept on watching the entrance gate of the college desperately. But time passed and there was no sign of a visitor or passerby anywhere in the college premise. Seized with panic and fear, I closed my eyes and divested my mind of all thoughts. If my prayers could not reach Swami, it must have been my fault. Perhaps there was not enough intensity in my words or transparency of feeling to move the Lord of the universe. I plunged inevitably into the slough of despondency and the morass of despair. And I resigned myself to my fate. 'Whatever has to happen... will happen,' I said to myself. I remembered the line of a French song which I had heard at an opera in Paris and it seemed to arm me with a sense of stoic acceptance of reality. I must subject my will to the will of the divine. There was hardly any respite from the mounting pressure on the brain and I lost consciousness for a while. As I regained consciousness, it seemed to me that the sound of temple bells rang all round and the fragrance of scented incense drowned my senses in a sweet stupor. I heard a voice calling me. 'Get up, sir, what are you lying here for?' I opened my eyes and found an unknown face peering at me with great concern.

'I have probably suffered a stroke. I have been lying here for hours. Now that you have come, I see a ray of hope for myself,' I muttered.

'Yes, I'll do all I can for you. I am an assistant in the university. I had been away to my home town and have arrived here just now. I was on my way to attend the function at the stadium. It sounds strange and unbelievable. It really does. Sir, as I was walking past the college gate, a voice rang in my ears, "Go inside the college... please." The voice was gentle, sweet and persuasive, but at the same time, it was compulsive and urgent like a directive, almost a command. So here I am, and am amazed to find you so terribly sick,' the stranger said. He leaned over me and tried to give me a prop to sit.

'No, no, let me keep myself stretched on the ground. You better rush to the stadium and inform the Vice-Chancellor or my colleagues in the Department and arrange to get the hospital ambulance. I need hospitalisation anyway, I am still in bad shape,' I muttered feebly. But the very next moment I had second thoughts. I feared to be left alone. The presence of the stranger had given me confidence and a sense of protection. So I said, 'I am not feeling quite well. Please take me to my apartment where I can rest. You can get some conveyance near the bus stand.'

He moved instantly towards the main gate. I was once again left alone to ruminate over my lot and I believed firmly that it was Swami who had answered my prayer and had sent timely help. The stranger returned within five minutes and informed me that he had brought a rickshaw.

'Please give me support so that I can stand up. You come on my right side so that I can put my right arm around your shoulder,' I whispered.

It was not much of a problem to walk. Leaning on my right feet, I took a few steps forward and dragged the affected left foot somehow. Descending a couple of stairs, I came on to the level ground in the college compound. I cast a glance at the flowers and the shrubbery and at the vast, limitless sky above the hills, lit up by the bright rays of the sun. With the help of the stranger and the rickshaw-puller I managed to board the rickshaw and heaved a sigh of relief as the rickshaw moved on the familiar street lined by the shops and restaurants doing brisk business as usual. A few buses bound for Dharmavaram and Bangalore were standing at the terminus. I felt comforted to hear the kindred clamour of the marketplace and to witness the scenario so dear to me, particularly the regal and magnificent building at the top of the hill which housed the central office of the university and the sacred dome of the temple on the *Ashram* premises. The rickshaw took a turn to the right and stopped in front of the three-storeyed building where the teachers lived in similar apartments irrespective of their position and rank. As my apartment was on the ground floor, I did not face any particular difficulty in getting into my bedroom. I was utterly exhausted and mentally nervous and disconsolate. The stranger helped me stretch out on my bed and asked in a soft accent, 'Is there anything you want, sir? Water?'

'Oh, yes. Look there in the almirah. You will find some medicines. I need to take the drugs for hypertension. Give me *Ciplar* 40 and *Adelphine Esidrex*,' I said. He gave me the

medicines and brought a glass of water from the kitchen. I
swallowed the pills and fondly hoped that any further rise in
my blood pressure would be arrested. I remembered the words
of my family physician and friend, Dr. A.K. Sen of Patna, who
had strongly advised me to take these medicines for life. It was
my fault that I had ignored his advice and missed taking the
drugs for weeks. All in all, I was rather complacent and
lukewarm about my treatment. Small wonder, therefore, that
I had to pay the price for my negligence.

'Sir, may I leave you now? I will be going straight to the
Hill View Stadium and inform all concerned about your
sickness,' he said.

'Do, please. Also make it a point to inform my wife and
daughter. More than anything else, I need their presence here
as I am feeling faint and drowsy, ready to slide into the
avenues of sleep and oblivion,' I spoke with a conscious effort.

'I will do all that you want me to do, sir. But for God's sake,
keep yourself awake and alert. Pray to Swami for immediate
recovery. Since he sent me to help you in the hour of your need,
I am sure, he will cure you of this malady. Nothing is incurable
when the Lord is your physician,' he said in a voice full of
conviction.

'Thanks a lot. I'll see you again,' I mumbled.

The stranger left quietly and I lapsed into sleep... perhaps,
it was not just ordinary sleep, but the kind of sleep I never had
experienced before, sleeping in the broad daylight, unmindful
and oblivious of the old chaos of the sun. I had had my
intimations of immortality and the sure, but imperceptible
mercy of the saviour, and nothing else seemed to matter. I
marvelled at the coincidence that he had brought the unknown
assistant who rendered such invaluable assistance to me in the
moment of crisis when I was utterly defenceless, lying in a
stupor on a deserted corridor with no prospect of human
visitation until the morrow. However, even now my condition
was like that of a mariner who, after a shipwreck, had been
swayed and tossed by stormy waves down to a strip of soil in an
island and was not yet out of the woods. But I had no time to
think. I found myself face to face with the Lethean twilight
which meant inoperability of spirit as well as loss of waking
consciousness.

When I recovered from a long, interminable eclipse of
consciousness I realised that I was in a different setting and
environment. A group of doctors and nurses were standing on
both sides of my bed. I recognised Dr. Chari, the
Superintendent of Sri Sathya Sai Hospital, who was checking
my blood pressure. The transfusion of saline water into my
body through the vein in the hand was going on and I was
breathing pure oxygen from the oxygen mask. It must have
been late in the evening as the gathering dusk darkened the
environment. I noticed the mark of twilight in the fields which
was visible from across the window pane in the hospital room.
But where was my wife? I wondered. I surveyed every corner
of the cabin.

'She has gone to get some milk and fruit juice for you,' Dr.
Kamala said. 'You must be feeling hungry. You have been
sleeping for the entire day.'

'Is it? But I am still very sleepy,' I said in broken accent.

'How are you now?' asked Dr. Chari with apparent
concern. 'You should relax and take it easy. The blood pressure
and respiration are within normal limits. Drive away all
anxious thoughts and stop worrying.'

'What are all these pipes and bottles for? Take them away,'
I said with great annoyance. I even tried to pluck out the pipe
and the needle from my right hand. Dr. Chari and the nurse
restrained me from doing so. 'Have patience for a few minutes.
Three-quarters of the liquid has gone into your body. In a
quarter of an hour the remaining liquid will also go. It will give
you strength and steady your nerves,' Dr. Chari spoke
genially.

I heard the sound of shuffling footsteps and was relieved
and curiously comforted to see my wife and daughter entering
the room with a Thermos flask in hand. Even during the
moments of desolation and hopelessness I had dreamt of them
and had nearly died a thousand deaths, thinking that I would
never see them again. I noticed the shadow of anxiety hovering
over their faces and I knew that the anxiety was all for my
sake. A faint smile played on my lips, a token of my gratitude
to them. The awareness that they were so vitally concerned
about my well-being and suffered on my account filled me with
a sense of joy, and sublime and tender emotions surged within

me and a tear trickled down my cheek. On the advice of the
physician, I took a light liquid meal consisting of coconut
water, Horlicks and tomato soup.

Dr. Chari said, 'Have a good night's sleep. You will feel
much better in the morning. I'll see you tomorrow. Good night.'

The doctor said something to the nurse and left. The lights
were put out and silence reigned all over the place. My wife
came near my bed and put her palm over my head. But sleep
eluded me and desultory thoughts crowded my brain.

'Try to sleep. It's well past midnight,' my wife spoke in a
sibilant whisper. 'Where is Sambhavna?' I asked.

'She's in the hostel,' my wife whispered in a low monotone.

I did not quite understand why my mind centred on my
little granddaughter, who was a student of Standard II at Sri
Sathya Sai Primary School. Perhaps, during this phase of my
physical and mental desolation, I was inclined to think of the
problems that required urgent attention and immediate-
solution. The sands of time were running out and there was no
knowing what would happen in the future. Apart from the fact
that the girl was my favourite, I used to feel great concern for
her as she was a patient of arterial septral defect in the heart,
a congenital defect that could be set right only by open heart
surgery. I had been praying to Swami day in and day out to
cure her. I was told by Mrs. Kaul, the lady principal of the
school, that Swami was particularly kind to Sambhavna,
giving her *vibhuti* occasionally while she sat in the *darshan*
line; once Swami had taken her in his car to the hospital for a
check-up. When I spoke to Swami about Sambhavna and
requested him to cure her, Swami smiled compassionately
which was enough assurance, if any assurance was needed,
that the girl would be all right.

Round about midnight, Dr. Kamala came to the room.
Finding me still awake she decided to examine me and check
my blood pressure.

'Professor Sinha, why don't you sleep? The more you sleep,
the better it will be for you. The trouble with the human mind
is that it manages to work overtime and plagues itself by
continual thinking. The result is that tension fills the blood
stream and complications arise. You should not worry so
much. Everything will be all right... all manner of things will

be set right. Swami is very much concerned about your sickness. This afternoon, he found time to speak to Dr. Chari and the team of doctors. I was also there. He expressed his displeasure over the fact that medical aid was not given to you in the morning itself when you had suffered the stroke. Professor Nanjundaiah and some of your colleagues in the Department had reported to the doctor in the forenoon, but they were asked to bring you to the hospital for admission and treatment at 3 p.m. in the afternoon when the oxygen tent and other facilities should have been made available then and there. We all felt very guilty and ashamed of ourselves. Swami spoke very feelingly about you. He has asked some of your students to look after you and provide relief to Mrs. Sinha. What touched me most is that he directed Mr. Gopal, a very competent, sober and gentle person, who has lived in Canada and worked as a male nurse in a hospital in Canada, to serve you and attend on you. Mr. Gopal will be seeing you on the morrow. He will give you good company as he is a warm-hearted and immensely lovable personality. Besides, he is a very good devotee of Swami and makes it a point to visit Prasanthi Nilayam once a year in November at the time of the birthday celebrations and stays on until Christmas or New Year. This time he has prolonged his stay for reasons best known to him. Maybe, he has been singled out to do this duty for you. How mysterious and inscrutable are the ways of Swami! He gives you suffering with a divine purpose so that you are cleansed and purified, and march, devoted and concentrated in purpose, on the spiritual path, the highway to God. So, do not worry, the present calamity will actually be a blessing in disguise to spur you on to deeper meditation and *sadhana* for a further union and deeper communion with the divine.

Dr. Kamala spoke with sufficient warmth and conviction in her voice. Then, turning towards my wife, who was listening to her with rapt attention she said, 'Mrs. Sinha, if you are fortunate to get near Swami in the *darshan* line, don't forget to seek his blessings for the early recovery of your husband. And, of course, let your earnest prayers mount up to him. That is the only way one can move the compassionate lord to shower his grace upon the suffering patient.' Dr. Kamala's face lit up with a glow. In fact, all those who had chosen to live at the *ashram*, leaving behind the cosy comfort of hearth and home to serve at the feet of the Lord, sincerely believed in the divinity of Swami and loved to speak about it more often than not. Indeed, the love for Sri Sathya Sai Baba bound all the devotees together in one volume.

My wife nodded wistfully. Since her devotion to Swami was as profound and soulful as anyone else's, she needed no advice.

She said in a serene and intimate tone, 'What else have I been doing, madam, ever since the morning when I saw my husband in such desperate straits? Prayer has been my only resource. I have been praying continually and shall be praying all night and forever more. I will surely speak to Swami as soon as I get an opportunity. Although I know that we ourselves are responsible for our suffering... for all that we have done and been in our innumerable *avatars* and our past *karma* and continue to suffer till such time as our *karma* is burnt out and we finally merge with the divine. Swami has said time and again that he is not the one who inflicts sufferings on us... rather he is a detached observer, the eternal witness. But if he chooses he can bring immediate relief and redemption not only from sorrows and afflictions but also from the cycle of births and deaths.'

'All you say is very true, but human aspirations prompt us to beseech the mercy of God in the moments of crisis. Okay, I guess I should be going as I have to attend to certain cases in the ward. You may be knowing that Dr. Alreja's wife is lying in a very critical condition in the room next door. Let Professor Sinha sleep,' Dr. Kamala turned round to go.

I remember vaguely that my responses were not quite sharp and my thinking not clear and transparent. My voice faltered as I tried to speak and was just able to pronounce words rather feebly and had to rely on the use of monosyllabic words. Even my vision seemed to have been fairly impaired. My perceptions, though they were not as acute as they had been in the morning when I was confronted with the crisis and danger and had fought hard for self-preservation and survival, remained reasonably coherent. I understood everything and comprehended the meaning of the spoken word, but was sadly incapacitated when it came to holding a meaningful colloquy with anyone. The words of Dr. Kamala came to me in a jumble and I vaguely surmised that she was speaking about Swami and trying to cheer me up. The insistent sound of the groans of a patient disturbed the stillness of the night and the faint moonlight seemed to weave a pattern on the glass panes and the walls of the building. For several days, I do not remember how many, I remained in a trance-like state, restless and frightened, deeply apprehensive that the fork of death might catch me unawares. Oblivion beckoned me tantalizingly so as to drown me in a sweet stupor and take me inevitably to its magical region of forgetfulness. I cannot relate the events of those twilight days and hours for all those details have been erased from the tablet of my mind. But as day broke after a long interminable night of shadows I woke up one morning in a stable and luminous frame of mind. It was indeed a glorious dawn, neither cold nor warm, but entirely sun-soaked and fairly breezy. My sensitive intelligence was again at work, everything about me seemed normal. However, in spite of the revival of the mind and the spirit, the dark night of the body was all about me. Though I could move my right hand and feet at will, the left leg and hand lay quite limp. Thus I lay confined to my bed with my eyes wide open and dreaming of all my life of action and sprightly and energetic movements that had taken me to far away countries on the European continent and the United States, the streets of London, Paris and New York, not to speak of ceaseless and frequent journeys to the Indian cities when life itself seemed to be a never-ending pilgrimage. I have never imagined that the feet that trod the pavements of innumerable cities, hallowed towns and sacred places of worship and lovely beauty spots would be rendered inoperative and non-functional. My enemy, death, had wrought this revenge upon me because I had not allowed it to hold its dominion over me. But this is perhaps the wrong way of putting it. Like John Donne, I had negated the sure and certain sway of death:

> Death be not proud, though some have called thee
> Mighty and dreadful, for, thou art not so,
> For, those, whom thou think'st, thou dost overthrow,
> Die not, poore death, nor yet cans't thou kill me.

From rest and sleepe, which but thy pictures bee,
Much pleasure, then from thee, much more must flow,
And soonest our best men with thee doe go,
The rest of their bones and soul's deliverie.
Why swellst thou then...
One short sleepe past, we wake eternally,
And death shall be no more: Death, thou shalt die.

Death, be not Proud

However, it had affected my movement and left the mark
of palsy on the left portion of my body. But I believed
passionately and firmly in the love and compassion of the Lord
of the universe and His power to heal me entirely and redeem
my suffering. So, on that glorious dawn I was fairly optimistic
and hopeful, my physical incapacity notwithstanding. As I
mused over the events of the past several days, I heard a voice
greeting me.

'Om Sai Ram.' It seemed to me as though the whole room
and the air was full of this auspicious greeting. The nearby
hills returned the echo of the saluting voice 'Om Sai Ram.' The
blue, azure sky, the delicate air, the rustling leaves of the
trees, the blossoming flowers all seemed to chant the self-same
greeting 'Om Sai Ram.'

I raised my eyes and saw an elderly person in spotless
white trousers and shirt and a scarf of fine silk, of light orange
colour tied round his neck which was the insignia of the Sri
Sathya Sai Sewa Dal. His face was mellow and the eyes fairly
compassionate and serene. I muttered, 'Sai Ram', and waved
my right hand as a gesture of welcome.

My wife stood nearby with a Thermos flask which she had
brought from our apartment or the *ashram* canteen. She
poured the tea into two cups and offered a cup to me and the
other to the visitor.

I had not yet brushed my teeth or washed myself. But I
was used to having bed tea and relished it greatly and it may
not be wrong to say that my day began with it.

The visitor smiled affably. 'Thank you,' he said. 'But first
let me introduce myself. I am Gopal, a resident of Canada. But
you will see from my face that it is brown and baked like that of
an Indian. Yes, do not mistake me for a Canadian. I am an
Indian by origin, but am domiciled in Canada. My forefathers

migrated to Canada way back in the nineteenth century. By
profession I am a nurse, doing service to the suffering
humanity. I have been a devotee of Sri Sathya Sai Baba ever
since the Sai movement began in the American continent.
Baba has shown me some tokens of his divinity by way of
dream images and the sprinkling of *kumkum* and sacred ashes
on his photographs placed in my worship-room. I am a regular
visitor to Prasanthi Nilayam and God willing, I might
eventually settle down here. Canada is of course, a glamorous
country, full of all material resources, power, and comfort. But
it does not hold me anymore. That world of material prosperity
is too much with me, anyway! And I pine for things spiritual,
for the warm, nourishing womb of the mother earth, the soil of
my country, the yellow fields of mustard, the merry dance of
the peacock when the clouds gather up in the sky, and for the
lotus rising quietly and gently in a sun-drenched pool. What is
more, I yearn to live in the divine presence here at the
Nilayam. I have prayed to Swami and have tried my best to
live up to his commandments. You know, Swami says, '*Manaw
Sewa* is *Madhav sewa*' (Service to mankind is service to God).
Doesn't he? And for full twenty years I have worked
steadfastly as a male nurse at a large hospital in Canada. If
Swami so desires and rewards me for my selfless service to the
sick and the wounded, I would like just one boon, that is, a
voluntary service as male nurse at Sri Sathya Sai Hospital.'
The visitor completed his long, but interesting introduction.

My wife was looking admiringly at him. And I remembered
that only the previous night Dr. Kamala had made a casual
mention of this man.

Mr. Gopal paused for a while and drinking the tea, said in
soft accents, 'Do I tire you by my uncalled for account of
myself? But, to make my narrative short, let me tell you that I
am here in this sick room with a mission. Swami has assigned
me the duty of attending on Professor Sinha on mornings and
evenings. "Make good use of your sojourn here, Gopal. If you
look after Professor Sinha and be of some service to him, you
will receive the blessings that come from a noble mind and a
beautiful soul. I shall be mightily pleased if you keep him
company and cheer him up. He has been going through trying
times and needs to pool all his resources to face the ordeal,"

said Swami yesterday, when he was speaking to the doctors about Professor Sinha. So, here I am! Mrs. Sinha, please give me his safety razor. It seems he has not shaved for nearly a week. And some tepid water as well. Also bring a towel, *kurta* and *pyjama*. I hope he is well enough now and can be taken out to the terrace on a wheelchair. Such outings in the mornings and evenings will do him a world of good. It's the mental resilience that is the essence of things. While palsy shakes the body, it is the paralysis of will that grips the mind.'

My wife brought all the items which he had asked for. Mr. Gopal applied himself to his job with cool efficiency. He shaved me in a fairly smooth fashion, wiped my body with a sponge and changed my dress. My wife put some hair oil on my hair and combed my hair. Mr. Gopal went out of the room and within five minutes he came back with a wheelchair. Since I was not in a position to sit up in bed by myself and transfer my body to the wheelchair, Mr. Gopal assisted me. 'First put your right foot on the ground and stand up with the help of your right hand, putting it on the bed, then move a step forward. Do not worry about the left foot. If you give sufficient force and momentum to the right foot, the left one will automatically go forward. All you need is to station yourself on the cushioned seat of the wheelchair and then lift the inoperative left foot with the right hand and place it on the footboard. Try this method and it may well be your exercise number one. Paralysis is not taken as a dreadful disease in the West, for physiotherapy starts right from day one. Unfortunately, here at this small hospital there is no trained physiotherapist. Swami has in mind the establishment of a very large and unique hospital with the best instruments and competent foreign doctors... a hospital that will be ranked among the best in the world. The poor will receive treatment without cost and major surgeries like open-heart surgery and kidney transplant will be done. But at the moment, there is not much by way of physiotherapy. And taking him to Bangalore just for physiotherapy does not appear to be a practical proposition,' Mr. Gopal said.

'That's very true,' my wife said. 'We have sent a telegram to our son who teaches at a university in Bihar. But I wonder if he can come and stay here for very long. Whatever is to be done shall be done by us. It looks so difficult.'

'Have patience, Mrs. Sinha. Swami will arrange things without your asking. In any case, you are facing the situation with calm courage. This is what everyone is saying in the *ashram*,' Mr. Gopal said. Then, turning towards me, he said, 'Now Professor Sinha, begin your exercise. Transfer yourself to the wheel chair. Yes, that's fine and now we go to the sunlit terrace and breathe the fresh air down there.'

With conscious effort and with the assistance of my compassionate nurse, I sat on the wheelchair and made myself comfortable. He pushed the chair smoothly down the corridor and through a large and spacious hall and we emerged on the terrace.

'What a glorious day! Look at the bright landscape with the cluster of buildings in the background. You must have missed the lovely scenes of nature and the vibrant air!' Mr. Gopal spoke softly.

'Oh, yes. How good to think that one is a part of this landscape... of nature that gives us so much! For days together I have been a complete stranger from this scene torn away... almost detached from nature, the shadow of death and oblivion looming large over my consciousness. But I could not make myself absolute for death on that uncertain hour at dawn and I was resurrected from that twilight region and I am here once again to relish the exquisite beauty of a golden day, right back in the lap of nature, my love, my paramour... my foster mother,' I said with fervour.

Mr. Gopal smiled and asked, 'How well you put it, Professor! Are you a poet?'

'In a way, yes. But I am not the kind of poet who writes poems. But I do see as the poet sees, the simple in its inexorable complexity and the complex in its tantalising simplicity. People say that it is a divine gift to be endowed with a poetic vision. I do not know. To me, it seems to be a notion that has no basis in reality and has not been borne out by the lived experiences of great poets. The poet, being more sensitive than the average human being and possessing a more organic sensibility, records like a seismograph the slightest tremors of sorrow, torment and affliction, and bears his sufferings like a cross and a crown. Dante had his rage against Florence, the city that exiled him; John Keats lived painfully under the ominous shadow of death, suffering from consumption; and Shakespeare, too, transmuted his private agonies into something rich, strange and universal. Sensitivity is truly a curse, if you ask me. I would rather be a commoner and live the common run of a life of action rather than of contemplation and introspection,' I spoke in soft and sibilant whisper.

'Although poetry is not my domain and I am not the sensitive or brooding sort, I do believe that I have missed the greatest of boons that God has given to man—the power of insight and easy access to reality. And God loves the poets already,' Mr. Gopal said.

'I am not so sure, Mr. Gopal. In fact God has ordained suffering and crucifixion for sensitive hearts,' I muttered gravely and cast my glance at the vast bluish sky, made resplendent by the morning sun.

'Professor Sinha, why do you address me so formally? Mr. Gopal sounds much too formal and distant. I tell you, when I saw you for the first time, I felt an upsurge of waves of feeling in the placid lake of my heart. You reminded me of my brother whom I loved and lost in the prime of my life. He, too, had large, deep and penetrating eyes and was given to a life of thought. I shall be happy if you call me 'brother'. Aren't we inmates of the Sai family, bound together by the silken bond of love and fellowship?' Mr. Gopal said in an earnest tone.

'Gopal *bhaiya,* that's what I will call you from now onwards. Will that please you?' I said, smiling.

'It would be wonderful! Now enjoy the beautiful, open air scene for a change,' he said and paced up and down the terrace. After nearly an hour, I expressed my desire to get back to my room as the sun was now high up in the sky and the rays were getting hot and unpleasant.

The brief outing seemed to have dispersed the gloom that had enveloped my mind after the climactic encounter with death. Hope ran high, the hope of treading once again the sunlit avenues of life, of completing all the unfinished tasks that lay ahead. I still waited for the *darshan* of Swami and felt the urgency of seeing him face to face and of phrasing my prayers to him in metaphors of poetry and the language of the soul. But wouldn't Swami, being omniscient, know the central thrust of my heart and soul? Moreover, from my past

experiences of receiving his grace, I had come to believe that
he was omnipresent. But, at that time of uncertainty about the
future and the awareness of numbness and immobility of the
left foot and arm I had no option but to wait and pray for the
mercy of the Lord. At that moment, lying on my sick bed in the
hospital room, I remembered the beautiful lines of T.S. Eliot:

> I said to my soul, be still, and wait without hope
> For hope would be hope for the wrong thing; wait without
> love
> For love would be love for the wrong thing; there is yet
> faith
> But the faith and the love and the hope are all in the
> waiting.

Four Quartets—East Coker, iii, 123-26

These lines seemed to voice my own aspirations and
apprehensions. But I was not sure of my ardour and capacity
for complete surrender to God and to leave everything to Him.
I, of course, loved Swami, but loved him in his otherness.

That evening, as I lay on my bed in a fairly serene and
tranquil mood a strange kind of darkness came upon me. I
watched the distant facade of hills and trees all being rolled
away in the twilight hour after the sun had gone down beyond
the western horizon and the rumble of the wings of darkness
was distinctly audible. My mental emptiness deepened and I
waited for something intimate and unidentifiable, perhaps a
summon from the blue, a call from the prairie, that could
gather me to the artifice of eternity.

Hearing the sound of shuffling footsteps at the door, I
looked up and was surprised to find the familiar figure of Dr.
S.N. Saraf, the Vice-Chancellor of the university, emerging on
the threshold. Since I have always regarded him as a kind
person, I felt rather pleased to see him.

'How are you, Professor Sinha? You look in pretty good
shape this evening. We were all alarmed to see you struggling
for breath on the night of January the eleventh, but that's a
thing of the past. We have absolutely no doubt in our minds
that Swami will bring you round to normalcy and sound
health,' Dr. Saraf said with a genial smile on his face.

I listened quietly and whispered, 'I was indeed on the verge of a precipice almost on the point of going down-hill, but I prayed to Swami. Prayers, they say, move the Lord.'

'Indeed they do, especially, the prayers that come from sincere and pure hearts,' Dr. Saraf commented.

Then he asked, 'Where's Mrs Sinha? I have good news for her.'

'She has probably gone to the *ashram* for *darshan* and from there she will go to the primary school to see Sambhavna, our granddaughter. She will be back within half an hour,' I said.

'I shall wait for a while. But I do not see anybody around to look after you. At least for a week or so, you should not be left alone.'

'Mr. Gopal was here a short while ago. We spent some time sitting on the terrace, I in a wheelchair. He has gone to the canteen to get tea for me,' I said.

While I was talking, my wife arrived with a beaming smile over her face.

'Do you know how much Sambhavna loves you?' my wife said.

'First listen, the Vice-Chancellor has some good news to communicate to you. You can later tell me all about our darling granddaughter,' I interrupted. Dr. Saraf said suavely, 'Yes, Mrs. Sinha, it's news that will gladden your heart as it has done mine.'

'What is it, sir? I just can't wait to hear it,' said my wife with a little bit of impatience.

'Cheer up, madam, Swami told me this morning during a brief interview between *darshan* and *bhajan*: "I have not been able to visit the hospital to see Professor Sinha. Tomorrow after the *bhajan* session I shall go down there. He is feeling disconsolate. If you chance to see him this evening, do please inform him and Mrs. Sinha and ask them not to lose heart but face the ordeal with courage and perfect equanimity and poise. Ultimately, he will emerge much stronger and spiritually more luminous than he has been ever before and have an acquisition or two which he had never dreamt of before. In reality neither the patient suffers, nor the divine acts. It's all a necessary process of self-purification and crystallisation of spiritual motifs. And have you deputed Sandeepan and other students to do duty at the hospital during the nights, and look after the patient and, thus, provide some relief to Mrs. Sinha?" said Swami. I am breaking this news to you at his behest.'

I felt, more or less, sublime to think that my prayers were answered and my wish to have a *darshan* of Swami was going to be fulfilled. What more did I want? If my sufferings and travails can induce the Lord to show such concern for me and come to see me, I would rather suffer not for just one but a hundred lives and I would, thereafter, become absolute for death and greet death as a welcome companion. I recalled the lines of Rabindranath Tagore glorifying death: 'Death, you are my beloved, my kindred companion, my *Shyam samaj.*'

As for my wife, she was delirious with joy and a few tears trickled down her cheeks, 'Glory be to you, my Lord,' she exclaimed and, turning towards Dr. Saraf, said, 'Thank you, sir, for bringing such a wonderful piece of news.'

'I tell you, do not let this opportunity go by. Speak directly to Swami and pray to him for the speedy recovery of your husband,' said Dr. Saraf tenderly and rose to go. 'Well, Professor Sinha, keep your will attuned to the will of the divine. I will be seeing you again,' he said and walked out of the room. I rated him as a very genial and sympathetic person, human in his approach to things. Although he was not an outstanding intellectual and luminary like his predecessor, Professor Vinayak Krishna Gokak, he was at least as warm and affectionate as he was. For long hours in the night I kept on reflecting on my singular good fortune and on the certain prospect of seeing the resplendent face of Swami. By a strange logic, I was ready to rehearse the experience of the seventeenth century metaphysical poet, George Herbert, in his beautiful poem, 'Love'. But the roles were reversed. I was not the travel-weary guest visiting the heaven where God resided and he, like a merciful and affectionate host, welcomed me. It was the Lord Himself who had chosen to visit a wretched and suffering patient to console him and redeem his suffering like the saviour. But I was no less conscious of my limitations, sins and human insufficiency than Herbert was:

Love bade me welcome: Yet my soul drew back,
            Guilty of dust and sinne.
But quick-ey'd Love, observing me grow slack
            From my first entrance in,
Drew nearer to me, sweetly questioning,
            If I lack'd anything
A guest, I answer'd, worthy to be here:
            Love said you shall be he.
I the unkinde, ungrateful? Ah, my dear,
            I cannot look on thee.
Love took my hand, and smiling did reply.
            Who made the eyes but I?
Truth Lord, but I have marr'd them: Let my shame
            Go where it doth deserve.
And know you not, sayes Love, who bore the blame?
            My deare, then I will serve.
You must sit down, sayes Love, and taste my meat:
            So I did sit and eat.
                              George Herbert, *Love*

And I waited tensely and hopefully for the auspicious
moment for the visit of Swami. As the day dawned, Gopal
bhaiya came to help me in shaving and changing my dress.
The sun looked bright rising majestically from the east and the
morning seemed to be clad in a russet mantle. Word had gone
around the hospital that Swami would be coming after the
bhajan session was over. The doctors and nurses came on their
usual round earlier than they did on an average day. But this
was a special day. After having received the admonishment
from Swami for not attending on me immediately after the
stroke, they were specially keen on making amends by giving
the utmost attention to me. Dr. Chari greeted me warmly and
conducted a thorough check-up.

'I wonder why the blood pressure is not stabilising,' he
mumbled as though he was speaking to himself. 'I have an
idea. I may try aquapuncture and see if it energises the
drooping muscles,' Dr. Chari said thoughtfully to the team of
doctors who had come with him.

''Why not take Swami's advice? In any case, it's not we or
the vast resources of medical science that matter. Remember
the evening following the stroke when the condition of the

patient was so critical and almost hopeless? His blood pressure
registered 230/110 and there was nothing we could do to arrest
this phenomenal rise. Anything could have happened... a heart
attack or brain haemorrhage. He had almost been rendered
static and immobile on the left side and his vision too was
impaired. We kept a nightly vigil, praying to Swami and
Swami seemed to be indifferent. Only seemingly so, for
actually the prayers of Professor Sinha and the plaints of his
wife and daughter had not gone in vain. And lo and behold...
the saviour in orange robes appeared in the sick room and
fixed his gaze on his face and kept looking at his dim eyes for
five minutes. And we have seen how the patient opened his
eyes and was revived by the sheer magic of his benevolent
glance and by his life-saving grace. Slight fluctuation in the
blood pressure is no problem. Mr. Gopal has been taking him
out on the terrace and he has responded well to the outing. The
sooner he gets out of his tensions, the better it will be for him,'
Dr. Kamala spoke with assurance.

'Oh, yes. Swami must be consulted about the future line of
treatment. Do take his blood and send it to the laboratory for
testing blood sugar,' said Dr. Chari thoughtfully.

I was fully alert and listened to their conversation with a
great deal of interest. I felt gratified to learn that Swami had
already visited the sick room while I lay in a precarious
condition and had saved me from the jaws of death. When my
wife came back from the apartment with breakfast and a flask
full of tea, I asked her, 'You did not tell me that Swami had
come here on the next morning following the stroke and had
revived me. Why didn't you tell me? I am dying to hear all
about it.'

'Take your breakfast. I will tell you all. I forgot to tell you
earlier as I was desperate and apprehensive and was crying
my heart out for your sake. I could not see you drifting down
the abyss, could I?'

'Even after Swami's visit and his blessings? It's really
strange. Swami blessed me and gave me the elixir of life and I
could not be absolute for death.'

My wife took out a few pieces of toast, fried beans and
cornflakes from the tiffin box and poured tea in a cup and
placed it on a table. 'Now tell me about Swami's fateful visit up
here,' I insisted.

'Your condition deteriorated very sharply in the evening. Your blood pressure, pulse rate and respiration caused great alarm and the doctors were at a loss to understand what to do. They thought of Swami and asked me to rush to the *ashram* to have audience with him. But the evening *bhajan* was over and Swami had retired to his chamber. Seated in the lawn in front of the temple I sobbed vehemently and invoked the Lord's mercy and grace and took a solemn resolve to move Swami by my tears and ardent prayers. I did not have a wink of sleep that night and kept vigil by your bedside. You were still unconscious when the golden rays of the sun peeped through the window. And then like a surge of ocean waves the lotus feet of the Lord of the universe appeared, filling all of us with ecstasy. Swami smiled serenely and straightaway cast a compassionate glance on your face. He looked straight into our eyes and you opened your eyelids, your lips moved. You whispered in monosyllables: "Swami! Make me absolute for death."

' "No, Professor Sinha, I am very happy with you and your work. You have still to do a lot of work for me."

'We all were greatly relieved and knew that Swami was truly the saviour, the absolute sole lord of life and death. But caught in the whirlpool of human delusion and *maya* I voiced my gravest apprehension. "Swami," I said, kneeling at his feet. "What will happen to me? Save the life of my husband and spare my *suhag* (marital state)."

' "Why do you fear when I am here? He will be all right and serve me for a long time," said Swami with a gesture of the hand and gracefully stepped out of the room. I was told that he had gone to the adjoining room where another patient, the wife of Dr. Alreza, was lying in a critical condition.'

I reflected on the information given to me by my wife and felt proud and blessed. The knowledge that Swami was pleased with me and my work seemed to set the crown on a lifetime's achievement. Surely I had got the affirmation that I was looking for all these days and when it came to me during my sickness it filled the vessel of my being with hope, love and faith.

Time ticked away, the clock time, that is... while I experienced a sense of timelessness, the bliss and the blessing of receiving a fraction of divine benediction.

My wife collected the plate and the cup and put them in a corner. Just then, there was a commotion and the noise of hurrying footsteps was heard. The door was ajar the next moment and the beaming face of Gopal *bhaiya* came into view.

'Swami's car has been parked below and he is expected to come here any moment. Professor Sinha, if you get a chance, do please commend my case to Swami. You just say that I have been doing service to you. I shall deem myself to be singularly fortunate if I am absorbed in permanent service at the hospital. I wish ever so much to return to India and my roots and spend the remaining years of my life at Prasanthi Nilayam under the benign shadow of Lord Sai.'

'Gopal *bhaiya*, I would indeed love to commend you as you have nursed me with tenderness and love, but Swami never wants prayer by proxy. You should phrase your ardent and sincere prayer with extreme delicacy of love and surrender and he will surely respond,' I said.

'Perhaps what you say is very true. Let me discharge the duty assigned to me with all my heart and the rest is not my business,' Gopal *bhaiya* said in a mellow tone.

Swami stepped into the room followed by Dr. Chari and other doctors. He scanned my face with his caressing glance. He materialised some *vibhuti* by circling his hand in the air and applied some of it to my affected left limb and gave some to me and said, 'Eat it.' I swallowed the sacred ashes. As I was aware of the strong medicinal quality of *vibhuti* I felt a sense of well-being and knew intuitively that Swami had granted a fresh lease of life to me. I had been successful in breaking the shackles of death and had become, in a different sense, absolute for death, for a kind of death in which one who dies wants to die again and again... a lifetime's death in love, ardour, selflessness and self-surrender!

2
THE NESSUS SHIRT: THE SHIRT
OF FLAME

Life is essentially pain-marred; some lives more so when one's destiny is to burn in the seething fire, the leaping tongues of flame and one can do nothing about it except bewail one's lot or move in measures like a dancer. This indeed is the human condition which is irredeemable, our common inheritance. When I recall and review the scenario and saga of my past misfortune and sorrow, I cannot help thinking that my personal and private agonies are very much a part of the general human predicament, not something imposed on me as an eccentric design by cruel and malevolent fate or as a consequence of the *karma* done by me in my past lives. However, if humankind faces this torment, there must be someone who has devised the torment. This has been a dilemma that has baffled me and no amount of reading and study of the scriptures and contemplation has helped me to reach the heart of the matter. However, in the course of my research on T.S. Eliot's later poetry I came across the beautiful fourth lyric movement of *Little Gidding* which seemed to clarify my doubts and confusion:

Who then devised the torment? Love
Love is the unfamiliar Name
Behind the hands that wove
The intolerable shirt of flame
Which human power cannot remove.

We only live, only suspire
Consumed by either fire or fire.

T.S. Eliot, *Four Quartets*, Little Gidding

Man cannot bear very much reality, but since he is born and has come to live in this shadow world of sorrow and gloom and is rooted in *maya* or illusion, he has to burn incessantly and forever. He *burns* in fire, the fire that is torment to the self-loving, purgation to the penitent, and ecstasy to the blessed. No wonder that Eliot in this great poem presented a masterly analysis of the human condition with the help of the beautiful and archetypal imagery of fire that kindles poetry into a living flame and charges it with a fiery glimmer, the extreme urgency of personal feeling and closes with mortal and immortal life united in the resurrection symbol of the rose of heaven. In the last quartet it is fire that dominates: the flaming glow of the sunlight on ice-covered tree; tracer bullets—the flickering tongue of the dark dove—the fires started by bombs: pentecostal fire, purgatorial refining fire, the fire of sin, the fire of love and finally the tongues of flame into a crowned knot of fire: the fire and the rose are one.

It follows from this that the only way to transcend the limitation of the finite human condition is to aspire for a merger with the divine and to see the vision of the Supreme Reality, the crowned knot of fire. Even earlier in *The Waste Land*, at the conclusion of the third section, 'The Fire Sermon', Eliot has assembled two passages, the one from St. Augustine and the other from Lord Buddha, to pinpoint the nature of human insufficiency:

To Carthage then I came.
Burning burning burning burning
O Lord thou pluckest me out
O Lord Thou pluckest me out burning.

T.S. Eliot, *The Waste Land*, The Fire Sermon

Eliot's attempt, like that of Lord Buddha and St. Augustine, is to trace the origin of evil and suffering in the world. The Buddha attributed all sufferings to the presence of passion in man and St. Augustine relates suffering and sin to the Fall. Since the paradisal man knew no suffering, the only way to redemption is to regain the lost paradise and the

burden of the human quest lies in the restoration of spiritual
health and vigour, and to move triumphantly to the city of
God.

But this is a condition which is difficult to achieve since it
requires the highest amount of spiritual discipline, ardour and
love. The *inferno* we live in, and the Nessus Shirt that we wear
close in around us are beyond human power to remove them.
Indeed the Nessus Shirt is our legacy and it continues to cling
to our bodies and sear our flesh like fire so that we, like
Hercules, die in wild agonies.

Hercules, the most famous of Greek heroes, subsequently
married Deinira, the daughter of Cenous of Calydon, winning
her by defeating the river god, Achelous, in wrestling. When
he and Deinira departed, they came to the flooded river,
Euenus. A Centaur, Nessus, carried Deinira across, and then
offered violence to her, whereupon Hercules shot him with a
poisoned arrow. The Centaur, as he lay dying, advised her
apparently with friendly intention, to keep some of his blood
which if smeared on a garment, would win back the love of
Hercules if he were ever unfaithful to her. And this Deinira
did. Finally Hercules attacked Occihalia and carried off Iole.
Deinira, to win him back, followed the advice of Nessus and
sent Hercules a robe smeared with the Centaur's blood. But
this, poisoned as it had been by the blood of Hydra or Hercules'
arrow, clung to his flesh and caused him fearful suffering.
                            Sir Paul Harvey, *Oxford Companion to Classical
                                              Literature*, 201-02

I quote these references with purpose. My suffering and
torment have been the result of too much of love. True, I have
been of human love possessed, and having been endowed with
a sensitive nature. I have either invited pain to myself or have
inherited it as my destiny. My maternal grandfather who
loved me very much, died when I had not finished my high
school education and I saw him depart to that bourne from
where no traveller returns. My father, who was still young and
a practising physician, breathed his last when I had just joined
the university. And since then, my life was one of ceaseless
struggle and continual sacrifice, attached to my unfortunate
family, my frail and defenceless mother and half a dozen
sisters and a brother to take care of. And I performed many a

noble deed that behoved the eldest son of a family. I entered
into an early matrimonial alliance at the behest of my mother
and such an alliance ensured that my younger sister got
married to a handsome and promising groom. And when I got
my first job in a far away city and later, in New Delhi, I made it
a point to take my sisters along with me so that they could get
the best kind of education. Furthermore, I took pains to see
that all my sisters got properly educated and happily married.
All this entailed constant worry and anxiety and heavy
expenditure. My travails were endless and my concern for the
family almost became an obsession with me, assuming the first
priority in my scheme of things. The result of all this was that
I could not do all that I needed to do for my immediate family,
my wife and two children. But fired by a strong sense of duty
and loyalty for all those who would die after me, I left for the
United States of America in the quest for knowledge infinite
and in the pursuit of my ambition. When I returned home after
the successful completion of my studies with the degree of
Doctor of Philosophy in English literature, I found myself in
the perilous seas once again and it was then that I was
baptised in misery and pain. First, my suffering was related to
my acute sense of despair, disillusionment and frustration in
relation to my search for a decent position in an ideal
university. I took my chances and appeared for personal
interviews at many universities throughout the length and
breadth of the country, but all my efforts came to naught. My
misery mounted in consequence and I showed signs of
hypertension appearing, and became very sick. God gave me
more sickness. The torment of unappeased ambition and the
sad spectacle of frustration made me very miserable indeed. I
felt I was confronted with a crisis similar to the one
experienced by George Herbert before he surrendered to the
will of God:

> When I got health thou took'st away my life,
>   And more; my friends die:
> My mirth and edge was lost; a blunted knife
>   Was of more use than I.
> Thus thinne and lean without a fence or friend,
> I was blown through with ev'ry storme and winde.
>   George Herbert, *Affliction,* 31-36

Next, I experienced the greatest shock of my life, an affliction that was indeed a bolt from the blue. So thorough and complete was my sense of affliction that it plunged me inevitably into the morass of utmost despair, a veritable nightmare, anxiety and doom from which I had no respite for nearly two decades. And it was the aftermath of that age of anxiety and perennial suffering that I received the fateful summons from the divine and I have hardly words to phrase my sense of blessedness and ecstasy. I can only echo the thought and feelings of W.B. Yeats:

> I am content to follow to its source
> Every event in action or in thought:
> Measure the lot; forgive myself the lot.
> When such as I cast out remorse
> So great a sweetness flows into the breast
> We must laugh and we must sing,
> We are blest by everything,
> Everything we look upon is blest.

W.B. Yeats, *A Dialogue of Self and Soul*

The crisis took me and my wife unawares. Our daughter R. (I will call her Rashmee), at that time barely fourteen years of age, suffered some sort of derangement of the mind. She had all the initial symptoms of the terrible disease commonly known as schizophrenia. She nearly lost her appetite and sleep, screamed in fright and rushed out of the house in panic. I watched her continually and took her to psychiatric clinics. The doctors diagnosed mental weakness and advised termination of her school studies and prescribed heavy doses of tranquillizers. Our life was never quite the same and we lived in a constant sense of anxiety, conflicts and tumult of the soul, sorrows, unpremeditated agonies and perilous adventures of faith into unknown territories. The critical dilemma that we faced shook the very foundation of our being and affected our very existence. My wife was a broken woman as she was the one who had to bear the brunt of Rashmee's crazy actions. At times, the girl turned violent and it became increasingly difficult for us to restrain her. During those dark days of tremendous misfortunes, I was serving at Muzaffarpur as Reader and Head, Department of English, University of Bihar.

Once when I had gone to attend a reception given in honour of
the visit of some distinguished American Professors at the
Vice-Chancellor's residence something unexpected happened
at home which shocked me and disturbed me for days on end.

When I returned home after the party late in the night, I
found the door locked. On hurried enquiry from the
neighbours, I came to know that Rashmee had run out of the
house in great frenzy and her mother had followed her
desperately. Perhaps Rashmee had gone to the railway
station, the neighbour's daughter said. I immediately rushed
to the station. One of the ticket checkers, who happened to
have been my student in the past, told me that my daughter
had boarded the crowded express train scheduled to go to
Lucknow. Her mother had tried her level best to dissuade her.
She even sought our help to get the girl out of the
compartment, but the train whistled and started moving. Left
with no other choice, her mother also boarded the moving
train, the ticket collector informed me. On hearing this I felt
nervous and frightened, as they had hardly any money and of
course, no ticket. They had gone to an unknown destination
without any purpose or resource. I returned home and spent a
sleepless night. The next morning, the first thing I did was to
see the Superintendent of Police, Mr. Ahmed with whom I was
quite well acquainted. Mr. Ahmed assured me that he would
send wireless messages to the Railway Police to each and every
station en route to Lucknow and assured me that my wife and
daughter would no doubt be traced. I thanked him, but my
anxiety for the well-being of my wife and daughter continued
unabated.

I squarely blamed my lot for the present predicament.
Friends and physicians had always advised me to get Rashmee
admitted into a mental sanatorium for intensive treatment.
Besides, her actions and behaviour had given ample evidence
of her deepening insanity and the prospect of something
untoward and calamitous happening any moment was very
much there. But my affection and concern for the unfortunate
girl who was the flesh of my flesh, made me oblivious to it all. I
would rather die than send Rashmee to live among strangers
or alien people or crazed patients in a sanatorium. But there
was no point in thinking about it all since the calamity had

already taken place. I fervently prayed to the gods to restore
Rashmee and her mother to me, but no news came for several
days. I lived in a state of perpetual misery and anxiety.

On the fourth day, I received a telegram from my friend
Dr. A.K. Srivastava of the Department of English, Lucknow
University, saying that *bhabhi* and Rashmee were with him
and would soon be going back to Muzaffarpur. So, the gods had
after all listened to my prayer. My joy knew no bounds when
the Lucknow-Gauhati mail train brought Rashmee and her
mother to the town and the sunflower in the garden blossomed
once again and the felicity was mine. However, my sense of
doom and depression plagued me as before, for Rashmee was
still in the woods. Sometimes, she would show a tendency
towards self-destruction by swallowing heavy doses of
Largactil or Melleril tablets or by trying to catch hold of live
electric wires. She, thankfully, seemed to have a charmed life
anyway and I wondered what I could do about it. I questioned,
like the existentialist philosophers, the very basis and purpose
of existence. I was indeed caught in a whirlpool and attributed
the human tragedy, my own personal tragedy, to the crisis in
the modern civilisation, to the nemesis of materialistic values
of life and to the loss of faith. The only way to redeem myself
and to get out of the oppressive and overwhelming crisis
seemed to me to lie in the recovery of faith and a return to
fundamental religious affirmations. The fact that my prayer to
the Supreme Force that presided over the destiny of mankind
and without whose consent not even a leaf fell, had worked
and Rashmee and her mother who had been safely restored to
me further replenished and fortified my resolve to meditate
and worship the Supreme Lord of the universe and appeal to
him to restore the normalcy of Rashmee's mind. Since my wife
was already given to a life of faith, worship and contemplation
and had extreme purity of mind and soul, she readily backed
my resolve to pin our faith in the divine for the redemption of
our unmerited suffering. However, in our new-found
enthusiasm and zeal, we ran after strange gods, *tantriks,
fakirs* and astrologers and miracle men, but were soon
disillusioned as there was hardly any improvement in my
daughter's condition. She had developed a strange kind of
fixation, almost an obsession, that she could shine as an

actress if she got the chance of joining films. She made a great
fuss about it and forced me to take her to the film world in
Bombay where I walked uselessly from studio to studio,
meeting some of the eminent directors. They strongly advised
her not to think of joining the film line, but to pursue her
artistic talent at home. I also consulted some eminent
psychiatrists who suggested that she could take a course in
dancing that would give her confidence and help her in
becoming normal.

Consequently, we took Rashmee to Madras and placed her
at Kalakshetra in a hostel where she could learn Bharata
Natyam under Mrs. Rukmini Arundale. However, this was
again a futile experiment, doomed to failure. Rashmee lived at
Kalakshetra for barely six months. In the seventh month, I
had to go over to Madras on receiving an urgent summons
from Mrs. Arundale. She told me that I should take the girl
back home and watch her carefully. In any case, she was not
cut out to be a dancer. Mrs. Arundale said that one day she got
terribly upset and threatened to drown herself in the sea
which was just a furlong away from the hostel. That precisely
was the reason why she had called me to take her back home.

Back in Muzaffarpur, life continued in the same familiar
rhythm of dread and peril and I was confronted with a deep
and abiding sense of nothingness. My belief in the philosophy
of existentialism deepened further under the impact of my
immediate experience. In spite of my best efforts, there was no
resolution of my genuine and critical dilemma. Rashmee
continued to be in her crazy moods, creating problems day in
and day out, and I continued to suffer the slings of an
outrageous fortune. No amount of intellectual exploration or
laws of thinking proved of any help and I was fairly convinced
of the futility of the human condition, the impotence of reason,
the bounding leap of the human being, estrangement and the
conclusive finality and immanence of death, solitude and
nothingness. In fact, I had come to realise that it was my
destiny to suffer and I was powerless to intervene.

I had heard a lot about two great saints of India, Deoraha
Baba who lived under a thatched roof, beside a flowing stream
and was said to be gifted with great spiritual powers... and Ma
Anandmayi who had an *ashram* at Varanasi. During my

official visit to Varanasi for a selection committee meeting at
Benares Hindu University, I took Rashmee along with me.
Deoraha Baba, at that time, was camping on the other shore of
the Ganges. As the boatman ferried us across the river, my
heart throbbed with nascent hope. Deoraha Baba looked at me
and remarked, 'So, you are from Muzaffarpur, aren't you? How
is Principal Mahendra Pratap?'

'He's all right,' I said.

'What brings you here?' asked Baba.

'My daughter. She needs your blessing,' I muttered.

'I know she is mentally weak. Please remember God.
Chant the name of *Rama*. Give your daughter the sauce of
amala that will keep her mind cool,' Baba spoke in an
affectionate voice. As the boat glided, gaily responding to the
splashing oars of the boatman, my heart responded as gaily. I
thought of Deoraha Baba who looked hoary and antique and
people believed that he was timeless and ageless. He had asked
me to chant the name of *Rama* and I resolved to do so, this
chanting could invoke God's mercy. Since God was shapeless
and without any tangible form, it was difficult for me to
concentrate. This problem was solved when I took Rashmee to
the sacred *ashram* of Ma Anandmayi. She appeared to be calm
and serene with a special aura of *ananda* or joy and bliss
sitting on her face. She looked at Rashmee with her deep,
compassionate eyes.

'Mother, you are all-knowing. Look at this girl, still in her
tender years. But her mind is not functioning normally. I
cannot tell you how much I suffer on her account... I who have
lived a noble and selfless life, loving and helping others. Why
has God given so much torment and grief to me?'

The saint's face was lit up with a divine glow, and she
whispered in soft, tender accents, 'The suffering is the
consequence of *karma* done in past lives. But you can turn the
tide by resorting to spiritual *sadhana* and remembrance of the
Lord.' Then, turning towards Rashmee, she asked:

'Do you believe in God? Which God do you like most?'

'Shankar,' muttered Rashmee quietly.

'Good. Then remember Shankar, not the form in which he
performed the cosmic dance, but Shankar in his calm and
tranquil mood,' the saint whispered in monosyllables and
raised her hand as a gesture of benediction.

Little did I know at that time, I was being directed to take the highway to God by some mysterious and unknown power. Now that I am at the lotus feet of Sri Sathya Sai Baba, the incarnation of Shiva and Shakti, I understand the great and full import of Anandmayi Ma's directive to Rashmee.

And the road to Prasanthi Nilayam was carved out for me subsequently and things began to happen as if in a dream, which has a strange logic of its own. It was then that faith broke into my life and I heard the summons of the Lord. I was preparing myself mentally for receiving such a call after the crucial and climactic experiences of the past several years and had almost lost my patience. Symbolically, the message was as potent, strong and unmistakable as the one received by Henry Vaughan, the seventeenth century metaphysical poet:

> God's silent, searching flight;
> When my Lord's head is fill'd with dew, and all
> His locks are wet with clear drops of night;
> His still, soft call;
> His knocking time; the soul's dumb watch,
> When Spirits their kindred catch.
>
> Henry Vaughan, *The Night*, 31-36

On the bright and sunny morning that followed, one of my girl students of the M.A. final class, came to see me. Fully aware of our predicament, she wanted to be of some help to us. She took out a photograph of a fair size, printed on a glossy art paper, and handed it over to my wife. She whispered with much warmth, intimacy and confidence, '*Bhabhiji*, place this picture in your shrine amidst the pictures and images of other gods and goddesses and worship it.'

'Whose picture is this?' asked Rashmee's mother.

'You may not have heard about him, but Sir must be knowing. It is the photograph of Sri Sathya Sai Baba who lives at Prasanthi Nilayam in Andhra Pradesh, South India. He is worshipped all over the world as God which truly he is, an *avatar* of Shiva. I am his devotee and have read all about him. Last evening while I was in my worship-room, singing a *bhajan* it seemed to me that a clear and distinct voice rang in my ear and directed me to give this photograph to you. And here I am at your service. If you worship him with faith and sincerity, you will certainly be rewarded, Baba says, 'If you take one step towards me, I will take a hundred steps towards you. If you give me love, my love and grace will flow towards you like torrents of a running stream and miracles will take place,' said the girl, named Sheila, with deep conviction.

My wife looked askance at me as she was fairly confused. She voiced her doubt. 'He is presumably a living person. How can I place his picture in the august company of Rama, Krishna, Ganesh and Durga? Wouldn't that be a blasphemy?'

'No, *bhabhi*, Sri Sathya Sai Baba is Rama and Krishna and all the gods who have ever incarnated on earth. He is all this and Supreme Brahman' says he, in categorical terms. 'You need not change or choose your god. Any god you might worship will not make any difference. In essence, it will be my worship. He is the absolute sole lord of the universe incarnated once again on this earth to spread *dharma* on a sound footing, to foster devotees and to bring the tortured and suffering humanity on to the ancient highway to God,' Sheila spoke fondly.

Sensing the dilemma of my wife, I said, 'Well, no harm will be done if you worship this photograph as well. People do adopt their guru and pay their obeisance at the sacred feet of the guru. In our tradition the Guru is Brahma, Vishnu and Mahesh, the Hindu trinity.'

By that time, Rashmee, who was listening to some musical records on the radiogram, came into the room and snatched the beautiful picture from her mother's hand.

'Sister, have you brought this for me? How handsome! Look at the curly hair resembling the tangled locks of Lord Shiva. I will keep it in the shrine and worship it. Anandmayi Ma had specially asked me to meditate on the sober and serene aspect of Shankar. Hadn't she, papa?'

'Oh yes, now go and put it in the shrine and seek his blessings,' I said cheerfully. It seemed to me to be a very auspicious sign as Rashmee, the patient, herself had taken a fancy for the picture.

And indeed, it was the beginning of a whole saga of redemptive and miraculous effects and actions of which I will speak in the subsequent chapters. The Nessus Shirt was still clinging to my body and it was verily an apparel of torture both

of the flesh and the spirit. A new element had entered my life,
faith and hope. My ardent spiritual longing led me on to the
contemplation of the divine essence and I nearly found an
anchor in the soul. My psychology was similar to that of John
Donne, expressed in one of his famous divine sonnets:

> Despair behind, and death before doth cast
> Such to terrour, and my feeble flesh doth waste
> By sinne in it which it' t'wards Hell doth weigh:
> Onely thou art above, and when towards thee
> By thy leave I can looke, I rise again,
> But our old subtle foe so tempteth me,
> That not one houre myself I can sustaine;
> Thy grace may wing me to prevent his art,
> And thou like Adamant draw mine iron heart.
>
> John Donne, *Thou hast me and*
> *shall thy worke decay?* 6-4

And Richard Crashaw's insistence on faith seemed the
only means to exist in a near impossible situation:

> Faith is my skill. Faith can believe
> As fast as love new laws can give.
> Faith is my force, Faith strength affords
> To keep pace with those powerful words.
> And words more sure, more sweet, than they,
> Love could not think, truth could not say.
>
> Richard Crashaw—*Hymn in Adoration of the Blessed*
> *Sacrament,* 11-16

The photograph of Sri Sathya Sai Baba was at the altar in
our shrine and my wife knelt before the galaxy of gods and
burnt incense and we waited for something unique and
unexpected to happen. Rashmee was much quieter than she
had been for the past few months although she still insisted on
going over to Bombay with a view to getting a role in films.
One producer, Mr. N.C. Sippy had given her an assurance of a
role in his forthcoming films. I had met him in Bombay and
had spoken to him candidly about the problem of Rashmee.
Maybe, out of sheer compassion and sympathy for the
mentally sick girl, he had sent a note, just to please her
without actually meaning to give her a break. 'She would
better be off if treated at a good mental hospital for her

paranoid fixation. But, I will consider giving her a minor role if it helps her to get over her obsession,' the producer had said. This was the reason why Rashmee behaved more or less normally as she was fed on irrational hopes. However, her patience was getting exhausted and she started picking up rows with her mother and brother who was two years older than her. The peace of the house was once again disturbed. My son, who was quite sensitive, started feeling alienated from all of us and nursed a grievance against us that we loved Rashmee and had little affection for him. He gave vent to his resentment on occasions. I was reticent in expressing my affection and was misunderstood. We lived in constant anxiety for him. The Nessus Shirt became much too oppressive and tormenting to wear and I writhed in perpetual agony and distress.

And then another tragedy befell the family. My brother-in-law, who had distinguished himself as a top ranking sociologist in the country and had risen to the rank of Vice-Chancellor of a university in the State of Bihar, was found dead in his bedroom under very mysterious circumstances. His death did not seem to be a natural one and it raised doubts about possible murder by the forces hostile to him at the university. Be that as it may, I could not see my dear sister suffer. I myself was overwhelmed with a deep sense of loss since he was not only my close relative, but also a bosom friend from college days, a kindred soul, a friend, philosopher and guide. The phase of mourning seemed to be long and interminable. I was firmly convinced of the nullity and futility of life and came to believe that the existential encounter was fraught with peril and danger. I was confronted with an either-or situation—whether to take up arms against odds or surrender to destiny or end my life. Whether to send Rashmee to a mental sanatorium at a far off place like Bangalore or to put up with the daily torture, which keeping her at home necessarily entailed. As it is said troubles do not come one at a time, but in battalions and swamp us entirely, I faced a terrible personal disappointment as my chances for getting the chair in the Department of English at the university blew over. It was a very dismal and humiliating situation for me. All the forces inimical and unfriendly to me seemed to have worked out a conspiracy against me and I was not selected for the post of Professor that should normally have been mine. I had worked so sincerely and conscientiously to put the department on the all-India map even as Reader and Head. I felt quite forlorn and miserable and lost my zest for life.

Unable to put up with the ignominy, I decided to leave the university for a few years and set about working towards that end. I was dogged persistently by bad luck and cursed my destiny. My wife who had been a continual source of strength for me during my days of felicity and adversity alike, was like a broken reed now and kept indifferent health. She became a victim of a serious disease, attacked by some unearthly germ or infection and was advised a complete rest for three months. However, she kept worshipping in her shrine and chanting her sweet and melodious *bhajans*. She had many beatific visions and dreams which sustained her abiding faith in the divine. It is a universal truth that women have instinctive faith and are prone to believe and surrender by the intuition of their pure and unaffected hearts and soul whereas men, on account of their self-love and intellectual outlook, murder to dissect and cannot surrender easily to any force outside themselves, even if that force be God.

And we meet the familiar compound ghost of our own being; so while my wife was achieving a difficult equipoise after having gone through the most trying and gruelling experience on account of her willing surrender to the powers that be, I was burnt in the flames of hell. I realised my own inadequacy, my failure to shed off my pride and self-love. Hence, on all fronts, family, job, art and God, I had tasted defeat and disappointment. As it has been said:

> At last, the rending pain of re-enactment
> Of all that you have done and been; the shame
> Of motives late revealed, and the awareness
> I have done and done to other's harm
> Which once you took for exercise of virtue
> Then fool approval stings.
> From wrong to wrong the exasperated spirit
> Proceeds, unless restored by that refining fire
> Where you must move in measure like a dancer.
>
> T.S. Eliot, *Four Quartets*, Little Gidding, i, 138-46

However, the concept of purgation, which is essentially a
Christian one is not common to Indian thought and philosophy
and, therefore, hardly relevant to my existential situation. The
Christian existentialists like St. Augustine, Pascal and Soren
Kierkegaard subscribe to the notion of existence and human
freedom for making a choice. The condition of human finitude
is explained in terms of original sin, as it is done in terms of
estrangement by non-Christian existentialists like Karl
Jaspers, Jean Paul Sartre and Martin Heidegger, whereas in
the Upanishadic and Buddhist thought the real reason for
human finitude and consequent estrangement from God lay in
the lack of self-knowledge. So my need at the moment was to
achieve harmony with nature and wait for illumination and
not for exposing myself to the flames of purgatory. I seemed to
reject the Catholic beliefs which get beautiful poetic rendition
in some of the greatest religious poetry from Dante to Eliot,
especially in *The Purgatorio* and *Little Gidding*:

The dove, descending breaks the air
With flame of incandescent terror
Of which the tongues declare
The one discharge from sin and error.
The only hope, or else despair
Lies in the choice of pyre or pyre—
To be redeemed from fire by fire.
T.S. Eliot, *Four Quartets*, Little Gidding, iv, 200-07

Paul Tillich affirms that the existentialist element is the
root and foliage of all theology and religious thought. It
appears somewhat strange that a philosophy like
existentialism with its doctrines of definite choices and final
commitments provides the one attitude that is common to
Christianity and to Indian thought, both Upanishadic and
Buddhistic. And the Christian existentialist's insistence on
knowledge of oneself is recurrent in all branches of Indian
philosophy and religious thought. Only through a process of
self-exploration can one attain the knowledge of *Atma* and the
Supreme Reality which are one, although we mistake the
illusion for reality, the rope for the serpent. Such a belief was
so deeply embedded in my consciousness that it attributed all
my suffering and misfortune to refractory vision and the

failure to know myself and the ultimate destiny of the *Atma* which is to merge with the *Paramatma*. So, I set out on a voyage of self-discovery so that I could get even a fraction of God's love and grace. Assuming that it was not within human powers to remove the Nessus Shirt, i.e., the shirt of flame clinging to the flesh, one could at least move to a condition of complete simplicity and total surrender to the Divine. This seemed to me to be the only way to transcend one's suffering and live in the enchanted radiance of God's love. This was an exercise that might cost not less than everything. But this, I thought, was as good a time as any to try to make a beginning.

The first condition for this was to cultivate detachment from self, from things, and from persons and to meditate on the Absolute Lord of the universe and to perfect oneself in the will of the Divine and hope to achieve the wished-for serenity and equipoise of mind so that it might become easy to take both joys and sorrows, pleasure and pain with an equal mind. On account of my general upbringing, sceptism and scientific temper, I had never been a person of ardent faith or a believer. Of course, I did possess some kind of provisional faith, faith in the prowess and splendour of the human mind and its power to create monuments of unageing intellect, permanent and timeless works of art. Having been a student of literature and gifted with a creative imagination of some sort, I had consecrated my life to writing and trying to know all about life, and transmute that knowledge into works of art. But the terrible reality of the mundane world had impinged itself on my consciousness in a colossal manner and I had nearly come to a dead end. Now it was time for me to break the knot of that tangled web or eccentric design and march to a new kind of freedom where the Lord of the universe could be my mentor and guide.

Under the new dispensation in the Department of English at the university, my discontent and humiliation continued as the person holding the chair happened to be a rankly mediocre, shady and scheming sort of person. Since he could not match me in any sphere—as teacher, scholar or man—he developed some sort of jealousy and animosity towards me. My cup of misery was full and I wished to escape to some other place for a short while. I prayed in the shrine continually, forgetting my earlier aversion to ritualistic worship or temple going. I burnt fragrant sticks of incense and voiced my inmost thoughts, 'Lord, You are omniscient. Give me some welcome respite. The existential situation of life is hard to bear. Have mercy on me. Do arrange a job for me elsewhere. And, most important of all, restore the normalcy of Rashmee's mind. If ever I have done some noble deed in my life, I do beseech your mercy to redeem me from this fire by the fire of Your benign love.'

Then a very strange and inexplicable thing happened. It was a moonlit night and the rose-garden in front of my house was drenched with dew, and stillness reigned supreme in the environment. I smelt a faint but unusually sweet aroma, the likes of which I had never smelt before. It could well be the fragrant odour of paradise. So soothing and compulsive was its effect upon my tired mind and bruised senses that I lapsed into a reverie and the perception dawned upon me that I was not alone in the dim moonlight. Another presence, some unearthly visitor, was beside me communicating the magical radiance of his presence in concrete and unmistakable terms. The aroma I am speaking about seemed to sink into the central depths of my consciousness and filled me with a sense of well-being and divine benediction. I specially record this experience, as on my first ever visit to Prasanthi Nilayam a few months later, I smelt the self-same aroma in the actual presence of Sri Sathya Sai Baba. From hindsight and my frequent inhaling of this aroma, I can say this was nothing less than an intimation of Divine Presence, the visiting card of the Lord. Such a belief was further strengthened by the fact that the shrine where the pictures of gods and goddesses were placed with the recently acquired photograph of Sri Sathya Sai Baba also smelt of the same aroma. Next morning, my wife called out from the worshipping room in great excitement.

'Look, what a delicious and sweet perfume. And look, all the glass covers of the picture frame are covered with thick cluster of ash-like substance. Is it the ash falling out of the burnt incense stick? Though, I wonder, it is thin and white and has very soothing perfume.'

I was engaged at that time in typing the script of my novel and did not want to be disturbed. But the mention of the

miraculous appearance of ashes on the pictures was too great
an event to be overlooked. I rushed to the shrine and surveyed
the scene with reverence and awe. The perfume was
unmistakable and was of the same potency as the one I had
had the privilege of smelling on the previous night. Truly it
was an experience that put me into such an ecstasy as I had
not experienced for several years in the past. Was it an
indication of grace descending on us? Was it an intimation of
blessedness or immortality, announcing the advent of the Lord
in our house? And eventually, some more mysterious
happenings during the next few days gave ample evidence that
my hunch was true.

My wife had a harmless and benign sort of a mole on the
upper part of her abdomen, near the ribs. It started giving us
cause for anxiety when she complained of pain. I took her to
one of the surgeons in the local hospital. The surgeon who had
just returned from the UK with F.R.C.S. degree, advised
immediate removal of the mole as it might create future
complications. He operated upon her under local anaesthesia
and removed the mole and bandaged the wound. Back to our
residence, my wife tossed to and fro on the bed on account of
extreme pain and restlessness. She writhed in agony and I did
not know what to do, for the surgeon had not prescribed any
analgesic. I rang him up to report about my wife's condition.
He said I could give her some pain killing pills but there was no
cause for worry as the pain would soon subside by itself. But,
unable to bear the mounting pain, my wife moaned in distress.
Then, all of a sudden, the familiar aroma floated up into the
room. The room, the air was full of it. I noticed some thin and
whitish powder falling like raindrops over the body of my wife,
on her face as well as on the bandaged wound. She quietened
almost at once, relieved of her distress, and fell asleep. When
she woke up after a couple of hours, she appeared to be quite
fresh and cheerful. The medicinal power of the sacred ashes
falling on the patient from the vacant spaces below the ceiling
and from the thin air had been demonstrated conclusively and
without any shadow of doubt.

These were small hints and indications which initiated my
interest in Sri Sathya Sai Baba. I contacted the convener of the
Sai Samiti, Muzaffarpur, and went to the bookshops and

musical stores where I bought copies of *Sathyam Shivam Sundaram,* the first two volumes by N. Kasturi and some records of *Sai bhajan* including the record of a discourse by Sathya Sai Baba declaring the purpose of his advent as an *avatar* on earth in this trouble-torn age of crisis, and recitation of his *bhajan.* It was then that I grasped the full implication of the appearance of the *vibhuti* on his picture and the other miraculous manifestations. And I felt that I was on calmer seas as though the frenzy and the mire of the human blood no longer tormented me and the heat, the oppression and the tyranny of the Nessus Shirt had grown virtually non-existent.

However, it would be wrong to say that I had come any closer to attaining the bliss or the ineffable peace that passeth all understanding. Rashmee raved and raged at times, although the periodicity of her rages and tantrums had diminished to some measure. My son who was working towards his doctorate at the university by fits and starts gave me as much cause for worry as the stubborn and insistent insanity of Rashmee. In respect of my profession all my attempts to get a professorship in a good university had proved elusive and unavailing. While all my sisters were living, more or less, happy married lives along with their families, the younger one was in perpetual distress on account of the foolish and abnormal actions of her spouse who had thrown up his decent job and lived in virtual penury. The sister next to me, for whose sake I had entered into an early matrimony, lived in constant anxiety and was struggling hard to fight against unsurmountable odds, arranging the marriages of her half a dozen daughters and preserving herself from some mild but certain heart ailment. My mother was as frail and defenceless as ever and kept on worrying continually for her children. In sum, I was still very much in the dark woods where the straight path was lost and there was no secure foothold anywhere. In this situation, the knowledge that some divine power was at my back was the only thing to rejoice at. I remembered the beautiful lines of Shelley, which always had been a source of inspiration to me and sustained me during the moments of crisis and dejection:

Many a green isle must there be
In the deep sea of misery.
Else the traveller, pale and wan,
Never thus could voyage on.

P.B. Shelley, *Lines written on the Euganean Hills*

And the beautiful passage in the third movement of *The
Dry Salvages* in which Eliot transmutes the wisdom of the
Bhagavad Gita, that is the only wisdom one can hope to aspire
for:

At nightfall, in the rigging and the serial,
Is a voice descanting though not to the ear
The murmuring shell of time, and not in any language
'Fare forward you who think that you are voyaging
You are not those who saw the harbour
Receding, or those who will disembark.
Here between the hither and farther shore
While time is withdrawn, consider the future
And the past with an equal mind....
And do not think of the fruit of action.
Fare forward.

T.S. Eliot, *Four Quartets*, The Dry Salvages

I was doing my *karma* in a disinterested manner, without
caring for the fruits of action in order to wipe out the effects of
the evil *karma* that I might have performed in my past lives as
a result of which the Nessus Shirt or the shirt of flame had
clung so long to my flesh and had disturbed the peace and
serenity of my mind.

I received a telegram followed by a registered letter from
the Foreign Assignment section of the Home Ministry,
Government of India, New Delhi, informing me that I was
appointed Professor of English Literature at the University of
Kabul, Afghanistan. Initially it appeared to me to a bright and
welcome piece of news and I related it to my soulful prayer to
the Lord to offer some kind of a break to me to spare me from
further humiliation of serving in a subordinate position at a
place where not long ago I was the Head, and of playing second
fiddle to a person much inferior to me in merit. But on second
thoughts and mature and rational deliberation, I realised that
it was a ruse to remove me from the country of my origin and to

expose me to further difficulties in an alien country. Besides I was sure that my future prospects of getting a chair in an Indian university would receive a severe setback if I were to accept the assignment at Kabul. So, I finally decided to decline the offer and persevere with my luck here and wait for my chance. I decided to leave everything to Sri Sathya Sai Baba and launch myself on my pattern of spiritual exercises and meditation.

In consultation with the convener of the Sathya Sai Committee and with Sri Yugal Kishore Singh, the State president of the Sri Sathya Sai Sewa Organisation, I arranged *bhajan* sessions at my residence on Wednesdays. There were some very good and sincere devotees at Muzaffarpur at that time, most notable among them being late Sri S.P. Atri and his wife, Mrs. Atri, who had a heart of gold, transparent and pure, and the bliss of living in Godly love reflected on their faces. Each and every gesture of their body as well as every accent of their speech conveyed the ardour of their soul. And the *bhajan* sessions proved a resounding success since word had gone around that Baba's *vibhuti* appeared on the photographs and consequently, there was a heavy rush of suffering people eager to participate in the *bhajans* and collect the sacred ashes. Rashmee invariably sat throughout the recitations and took sincere and active interest in chanting the *bhajans*. Thus, the atmosphere in our house became charged with religious fervour. Among the miracles that took place with great frequency, the one that overwhelmed me greatly was the strange and inexplicable phenomenon of the electric lights and fluorescent tubes burning automatically in the shrine and the adjoining hall where devotees assembled for singing the *bhajans*. And the appearance of thick clusters of fragrant *vibhuti* on the picture of all gods and goddesses as well as large imprints of feet in *vibhuti* and *kumkum* surprised all of us.

Once it so happened that after the *bhajan* session ended, the assembled devotees came up to the first floor to take *prasad* and as they climbed the winding stair going up to the first floor, they were amazed to see imprints of footsteps on the stairs all the way, suggesting the certain visit of the Lord. It is often customary that whatever we do not understand or relate to cause and effect or explain away according to the rational

laws and principles of science, we call a miracle. Since I had an
empirical scientific temper, having the benefit of a liberal
English education in the West, it was fairly disturbing to think
that such a strange phenomenon took place before my very
eyes and I could not understand the 'why' and the 'wherefore'
of such happenings. 'Was it an imp or some supernatural
agency that was doing all this?' I wondered. But the more I
thought over it, the more confused I became. I had read very
extensively the Bible and the *Mahabharata,* and the
biographies and autobiographies written by mystics and
saints. The Christ as well as Krishna and other full or partial
avatars and *rishis* and saints had performed many a miracle
for human good. In Howard Murphet's *Sai Baba: The Man of
Miracles,* I had read the account of the miracles performed by
Sri Sathya Sai Baba, which proved his divinity conclusively.
To perform miracles was the second nature of the *avatar.*
These were performed out of sheer love and to ameliorate the
sufferings of devotees and to instil faith in God. But, as I have
mentioned earlier, I have not been a believer by nature or
temperament. I do not easily accept the reality of miracles or
romantic and outworm notions of immortality. On the
contrary, I am inclined to feel at one with the lady who is the
chief protagonist in Wallace Stevens's great poem *Sunday
Morning:*

> We live in the old chaos of the sun,
> Or old dependency of day and night
> Or island solitude, unsponsored, free,
> Of that wide water, inescapable
> Deer walk upon our mountains, and the quail
> Whistle about us their spontaneous cries;
> Sweet berries ripen in the wilderness:
> And, in the isolation of the sky,
> At evening, casual flocks of pigeons make
> Ambiguous undulations as they sink,
> Downward to darkness, on extended wings.
>   Wallace Stevens, *Sunday Morning,* viii

However, the indications as well as the descent of grace
seemed to be insistent and unmistakable and forced me to
revise my attitude of intellectual defiance or disbelief. And

God, on His part, was determined to drive home the lesson that man is but a reed, the most feeble thing in nature with limited knowledge and wisdom and that there was no way other than the way of complete submission and total surrender to the will of God.

Since my life was pain-marred and my suffering was stupendous, I was living in perennial tension and anxiety and could not tear off or remove the Nessus Shirt. I allowed myself to be swayed by the miracles so that the buds of faith blossomed in the barren tract of my heart. Naturally, any attempt to transcend my unlimited sufferings meant that I should look for some unique and precious annunciation of the indications that might put me on the sure and certain path of salvation:

I remembered, in this context, the lines of T.S. Eliot in *The Dry Salvages:*

There is no end of it, the voiceless wailing,
No end to the withering of withered flowers,
To the movement of pain that is painless and motionless,
To the drift of the sea and the drifting wreckage,
The bone's prayer to Death its God.
Only the hardly, barely prayable,
Prayer of the one Annunciation.

T.S. Eliot, Four Quartets II

However, the ordeal by fire was not yet over. Very soon I encountered the worst kind of crisis that shattered me completely and belied all my hopes and expectations. The tokens and emblems which I hopefully took as divine mercy and benediction turned out to be just a flash in the pan, just a bit of moonshine. Indeed, as the great poet has said through one of the characters in *Julius Caesar*:

There is a tide in the affairs of men...
The fault, dear Brutus is not in our stars, but in ourselves
that we are underlings.

I took a rather hasty and rash decision and proceeded to Shimla in Himachal Pradesh to take up a new assignment as a Visiting Fellow at the prestigious Institute of Advanced Study to work on my research project on 'Symbolic Configuration in Recent English Poetry.'

I was tempted by the prospect of living in Shimla, away from the nightmare of Muzaffarpur in the backwaters of Bihar which had been a place of disaffection for me... and a place of disillusionment and defeat. Everything happened in such a dramatic manner and with such swiftness that I was forced to decide in haste. Little did I know at that time that the decision was fraught with risk and that I was inviting trouble for myself. Besides, the miraculous manifestations in the house at Muzaffarpur should have convinced me that there was the prospect of grace abounding in not too distant future. I should have left everything to Sri Sathya Sai Baba, but instead, I had plunged into an unpremeditated action. While my decision to turn down the offer of Professorship at the University of Kabul was a wise and mature one, this one, taken in a hurry and prompted by a desire to escape the abysmal reality at home, proved to be my undoing. But I did not listen to the voice of my conscience. My wife had to stay at Muzaffarpur as my son was nearing the completion of his research work and he could not be left alone.

So, I went to Shimla with my daughter, Rashmee, and a boy servant. Initially, I was fairly happy and excited about my sojourn in Shimla. The Institute was located in the fabulous Rashtrapati Niwas. My office was large and spacious with costly furniture. My residence was a lovely three-roomed apartment on a steep ascent alongside the path to the famous Kamana Mandir. The surroundings were lush green and the horizons looked shining and silvery when the bright sun rays made the snowcapped peaks luminous. The scenario seemed very fascinating indeed and I observed the beauty of the landscape with relish and considered myself to be fortunate to live so close to nature. No wonder Shimla was the queen of the hill stations and the research project was challenging and ambitious enough to keep me interested and occupied. But on the negative side, the business of living alone with Rashmee and a boy servant posed many a problem. I had to devote much time to the house, preparing breakfast and lunch and looking after Rashmee who, after the initial excitement, was getting stale and restless. She forced me time and again to take her out for excursions to the Jakhu hills over the Mall, to the snow-covered regions of Kufri and to other beauty spots in and around Shimla. The thing that pleased her most was to wander along the Mall, eat in posh restaurants and to see movies and buy lots of musical records and magazines. I watched her with a sense of deep apprehension for she was showing symptoms of maniac depression. So much of my time was consumed in watching her with extreme anxiety that work on my research project became secondary. I longed to get back to Muzaffarpur where at least I could get emotional sustenance in the company of my wife and resume worship at the shrine. Obviously, I did set certain hints, but had missed the meaning and had escaped to Shimla in pursuit of a chimera. The moments of happiness had receded into some dark tunnel and needed resurrection through contemplation and exercise of memory and grace of sudden illumination:

> The moments of happiness—not the sense of well-being,
> Fruition, fulfilment, security or affection,
> Or even a very good dinner, but the sudden illumination
> We had the experience but missed the meaning,
> An approach to the meaning restores the experience,
> In a different form, beyond any meaning
> We can assign to happiness.
>   T.S. Eliot, *Four Quartets*, The Dry Salvages, 190-96

Since I had wavered in faith and had tried to arrange my life according to my limited and finite understanding and wisdom, the super-power made me suffer even more. The shirt of flame clung to my flesh more adhesively and closely than before, and any possibility of its turning into roses had receded for the time being.

To make a long story short, I must relate in a nutshell the calamitous event that took place in Shimla. Rashmee had insisted on going to the Mall to see a movie. Much against my wishes, I had to accompany her to the cinema hall. The movie was about the tragic life of an innocent girl who, like Tess, had been seduced by scoundrels and destiny played pranks with her. The cumulative effect of the movie on that late November night when the weather had turned extremely inclement and generated some sort of wintry fever in the nerves saddened me beyond measure. Rashmee was quite restless and upset. As we walked along the main street going from the Mall to

Rashtrapati Niwas, Rashmee started running, all of a sudden, with a loud scream. The deep ravines on both sides of the desolate street looked frightening and the track was empty. I had a hard time keeping pace with Rashmee and when I caught hold of her arm, she resisted and screamed in a terrible temper. There was a sanatorium on the way and the lights were on. I succeeded somehow in taking Rashmee up there. The matron heard me patiently, but she expressed her inability to do anything. 'Ours is not a mental sanatorium. Moreover, the doctor has gone on holiday to New Delhi. I am sorry,' she said apologetically.

After many hours of constant effort, including the use of force, I was able finally to bring Rashmee back to my residential quarters. But she raved and raged continually and the peace of the night and the desolate health was broken. But no one turned up to help me. I locked Rashmee in her bedroom and kept vigil anxiously the whole night long. I had no close friend or relative in Shimla with whom I could share my grief or seek advice or assistance in this difficult situation. Rashmee's occasional screams and the muffled sound of her spasmodic sobs mixed with the howling of the storm outside disturbed me and robbed the calm and poise of my mind. I blamed myself for all this and rued my decision to embark on an unnecessary misadventure in coming over to Shimla and felt as though I were in an island of solitude, unsponsored and defenceless. The houses of my other colleagues were on the other adjoining hills and even the doctor lived far away on Summer Hill. My boy servant was much too small and childish to be of any help. As I lay awake in the raging storm of that fateful night, I thought of the images in my shrine at Muzaffarpur and of the fragrant smell of an unearthly nature. Someone seemed to whisper into my ears: 'Retrace your steps and realise the rank folly of seeking fresh avenues and pastures new. You just cannot step into a new kind of freedom unless you surrender yourself to the Lord. Beware, you might lose your dear daughter if you stay in Shimla any longer. In any case, you cannot keep her on the leash during her rages.'

I resolved to relinquish my post at the Institute and took Rashmee for an extensive check-up and possible hospitalisation at Ranchi in the European hospital for mental diseases. The journey from Shimla to New Delhi and to Ranchi was troublesome and by the time I reached Ranchi I was nearly a ruined man. The Superintendent of the hospital was a genial and kind person and he strongly advised me to leave Rashmee for close observation and for a rather longish treatment. He assured me that her paranoia was not something complex or complicated. It might be related to her mental deficiency and consequent lack of confidence. 'Given ample care and affection, she might respond favourably. I will put her on tranquillizers and even on occasional electric shock therapy,' said the Superintendent. Something broke within me and tears welled up in my eyes. The calamity which I dreaded always and feared most had come to pass and my heart bled for the sake of Rashmee. I do not recollect how I suffered the agony of seeing my beloved Rashmee being taken forcibly away into the interior of the sanatorium by the matron and nurses and hearing her desperate and piteous cries, 'Papa... do not leave me. I promise I shan't misbehave but live peacefully at home.... Papa, please... give me a chance.'

The memory of her figure receding into the dark caverns of that hell where crazy women dwelt in the hope of redemption and recovery, and the loud lament voiced by Rashmee rang in my ears for many days. When I reached home at Muzaffarpur, I was in a desolate state, sleepless and fatigued. When my wife asked me where Rashmee was, I just could not make any reply. Instead, I was rendered dumb and shook with uncontrollable convulsions and tears welled up in my eyes as my mental emptiness deepened. Eventually I related all that had happened. My wife whispered sadly, 'Perhaps you have done the right thing.' I always believed in the need and urgency of doing the right action. All human efforts must be made. Only when one fails does God intervene and bring about relief. I tell you Rashmee will surely be all right by the grace of God. I have been getting intimations of this in my dreams. 'You must go to the university and rejoin your post as Reader. In your absence there has been a very sad and unfortunate event in the Department. The Professor has proceeded on a long leave for undergoing a surgical operation. He is presumably suffering from cancer of the liver, poor fellow. Strange are the ways of providence. He had the good luck of getting the chair here, but

now his very existence is threatened by this terrible disease,'
my wife said rather gravely. Being gentle and compassionate
by nature, she was always moved by pity for any suffering
creature. Whereas I had learnt to develop a sense of stoic
resistance to suffering and pain, she had much more the milk
of human kindness, which flowed unabated even for strangers.

I joined the post the very same day and received a letter
from the Registrar, asking me to act as the Head of the
Department of English as well, until further orders. I resumed
my work, but deep down somewhere in the heart, something
had snapped. I wondered how Rashmee might be living at the
sanatorium without us. I brooded for hours without end, and
although the work in the Department kept me terribly busy, I
could not stop worrying about Rashmee. In the evening I
booked a long distance telephone call to Ranchi and when the
line was available, I enquired about Rashmee's condition. The
Superintendent informed me that she was eating and sleeping
well and was calm and sedate after a couple of electric shocks.
When I asked him to give the phone to Rashmee, he advised
me not to speak to her at the moment, fearing that she might
be upset and start fretting about going back home and said
that I could speak to her later the next week when her
condition stabilised further. Anyway it was good to hear about
the progress in Rashmee's mental condition.

And I resumed my prayers and *bhajans* with an additional
zeal. There was some lessening of tensions and gloom day by
day and the situation in the place of work became, more or less,
congenial. The post of Professor was still vacant after the
tragic death of the present incumbent and the requisition was
officially sent to the Bihar Public Service Commission for
advertising for the post and sending their recommendations at
an early date. However, as the whole process was a time-
consuming one, it was expected that the process would be
completed over a period of four to six months. My son had
submitted his doctoral thesis to the university and was
awarded the degree. He got a break rightaway and
successfully competed for the post of lecturer at Magadh
University, Bodh Gaya. Thus, there was comparative peace on
the family front, although the absence of Rashmee rankled and
hurt in the sore spot the heart.

In the meantime, the signs and emblems of God's grace continued to pour in from time to time. My wife was the medium through whom the token of grace was communicated. Not to speak of the clusters of *kumkum* and *vibhuti* which were sprinkled on the pictures, there also appeared on the back of my wife's palm whenever she worshipped or chanted the name of Sri Sathya Sai Baba. This phenomenon was so mysterious and obvious that it could be demonstrated at will anytime, anywhere. During a visit to New Delhi to attend a meeting at the Union Public Service Commission, one of my old students, who was in the Indian Administrative Services, requested my wife to stand in the stance of prayer and *aradhana* before the portrait of Sri Sathya Sai Baba placed in his living room. My wife did so and, as usual, the back of her palm was covered with a profuse quantity of *vibhuti* and *kumkum*. We also attended *bhajan* sessions at the houses of devotees in New Delhi and visited the temple where the image of Shirdi Sai Baba was installed. I prayed continually for the speedy recovery of Rashmee.

And it seemed that God had listened to my plaint and prayer. On my return from New Delhi, I found an urgent telegram from the Superintendent of the European Mental Hospital informing me that the patient was keeping quite well and that it was time I could take her back home and arrange for her rehabilitation in society. I must say it was the brightest piece of news that thrilled me. I booked the train reservation for Ranchi and set out on my fateful journey to the underworld, to Hades, as it were. And it actually proved to be a descent into hell, like that of Dante or Aeneas, and once again, I found myself shipwrecked in perilous seas. Rashmee looked as calm as I had known her to be before her ailment. However, she looked dazed and morose. The Superintendent prescribed medicines to be taken for six months and advised me to keep her engaged in work. On our way back home, we decided to break our journey at Gaya just to see my son and meet some close relatives. We stayed at the bungalow of my brother-in-law. Unfortunately, Rashmee had a row with one of her cousins and she got greatly agitated. As I was very tired and fatigued, I slept soundly during the night, but in the uncertain hour before daybreak, I heard the sound of hurried footfalls.

My brother-in-law came in to inform me that Rashmee had slipped from the terrace and had fallen on the hard ground below. I came out to see her. She was groaning with pain and was unable to sit up or stand. I called an ambulance and took her to the Medical College. The Professor of orthopaedics examined her and admitted her into the special ward. An X-ray of the spine revealed a fairly pronounced crack in the first vertebra. She was put on a hard bed and advised complete rest for nearly six weeks. The Professor, who later became an ardent devotee of Sri Sathya Sai Baba late, told me frankly that the injury was pretty serious and the consequent monoplegia might well become a permanent condition, should there be a collapse of the cracked vertebra. He asked me to remember God and pray to Him, while he himself would render all possible medical assistance. Truly, this was indeed the greatest crisis which I had to contend with and I was torn and mutilated inwardly. It was not my fault that God had chosen to subject me to such a cruel, stupendous and heart-rending test. But His will would be done and I had very little say in the matter. The reality of the burning shirt of flame was very much there, almost turning out to be a conflagration. Nor could I take any comfort or consolation in accepting tragic gaiety like Timon or King Lear or the Poet William Blake who beat upon the wall till truth obeyed his call. Indeed blessed person, he!

I sent a telegram to the Vice-Chancellor of the university praying for six weeks' special leave and informed my wife about the mishap on the telephone. Having done this, I settled down to a close and continuous vigil over the unfortunate girl who writhed in pain. My son came to the hospital daily to be by my side, but his work at the college prevented him from staying during the nights. Other relatives made their formal visits, but I had to bear the agony of watching Rashmee's fluctuating condition. Her kidney and bowels were not functioning properly and she had to be taken to the intensive care unit for necessary observation and treatment. My nerves were on edge and I raged against a hostile and unfeeling God for having singled Rashmee out for crucifixion and for punishing me with unmerited afflictions of mind and soul. Darkness seemed to envelop me in its deadly pall where many menacing spirits and monsters peered at me. The poem of Archibald Macleish appeared to me to be so relevant in the situation:

> And there, there overhead, there, there hung over
> Those thousands of white faces, those dazed eyes,
> There in the starless dark the poise, the hover
> There with vast wings across the cancelled skies,
> There in the sudden blackness the black pall
> Of nothing, nothing, nothing—nothing at all.
>
>   Archibald Mcleish, *The End of the World,* St. I

3
THE ALL-KNOWING
FOUNTAIN OF LOVE

Rashmee's condition caused great alarm and anxiety as her nervous system was impaired on account of the fall. There was no knowing when the artery and veins would pick up the signals from the brain and would be regenerated. The orthopaedic surgeons wondered if it would be advisable to perform a surgical operation at this stage in order to hasten the process of regeneration. But there was a difference of opinion about it. So it was decided to keep the patient under strict observation. However, the pain had subsided and the catheter was removed. I purchased a number of magazines and novels for Rashmee to enable her to pass her time, while I brooded over my lot and uttered my prayers to God desperately. Never did a father love his daughter so dearly as I did, and never was love the cause of so much suffering and travail. I prayed to God either to bring immediate relief to Rashmee or else to better my heart. There was yet another way to transcend the suffering and that meant the stoic acceptance of the reality and for me to take the stance of tragic gaiety and wait for the dawning of truth, love, faith and grace. I longed for both defiance and acceptance, like W.B. Yeats:

> Grant me an old man's frenzy,
> Myself must I remake till I am Timon and Lear
> Or that William Blake
> Who beat upon the wall
> Till Truth obeyed his call;
> And again, hope to achieve
>   W.B. Yeats, *An Acre of Grass*, Stanza iii

Gaiety transfiguring all that dread,
All men have aimed at, found and lost:
Black out; Heaven blazing into the head;
Tragedy wrought to the uttermost.

W.B. Yeats, *Lapis Lazuli*, Stanza ii

After the anxious period of waiting, the Professor of
orthopaedics reluctantly agreed to discharge the patient from
the hospital and suggested that she should be lying on a hard
bed most of the time and go out for short walks in the evenings
by way of exercise, but she must fasten a belt around the waist,
covering the lower spine as a necessary precaution. Any jerk or
jolt must be avoided at all costs. When I enquired what her
chances of complete recovery were, the Professor, a genial and
kind-hearted person, said that it all depended on the grace of
God because a spinal crack would make the patient vulnerable
to all kinds of possibilities such as the collapse of the vertebra
and persistent pain in cold weather and the mal-functioning of
the nerves, even paralysis for lifetime. But if she was lucky,
she might be able to lead a normal life and do all her work by
herself. While most patients became permanent invalids, a few
fortunate ones managed to remain quite active. The Professor
hoped that Rashmee might recover completely by the grace of
God. I thanked him and with the help of the Superintendent of
Police, who happened to be my student at one time in the
Department of English, Bihar University, I got a reliable taxi
driver and set out for Muzaffarpur. Rashmee withstood the
strain of the journey fairly well and I called a reputed surgeon
to examine her and assess the extent of her injury. An X-ray
was taken and injections and medicines were prescribed.
'There are chances of distinct improvement,' said the surgeon.
I resumed my duties in the Department, and rest was prayer,
observance, discipline, thought and action.

It was then that divine intervention came about in a big
way and there were emblems of everlasting grace. *Vibhuti*
came directly from the air on a piece of paper or in an urn
which I had placed in the shrine before the picture of Sri
Sathya Sai Baba. I mixed the *vibhuti* in a glass of water and
gave it to Rashmee to drink. The container was again full to
the brim in no time. This continued for several days and only
stopped when Rashmee regained her strength and could stand

on her feet and walk with normal gait. Furthermore, I received an intimation for a personal interview for the position of Professor of English from the Bihar Public Service Commission, and thus Dame Fortune smiled on me and everything went my way. I was appointed University Professor and felt gratified that my ambition had been fulfilled, setting a crown to my career. I knew in my heart of hearts that some divine power helped me in a mysterious manner. Rashmee, too, was in a much better frame of mind and cooperated with her mother in domestic work and spent her time in watching television or reading light literature.

Peace reigned in the house, and the tortures and torments had become a thing of the past. My friends and well-wishers came to congratulate me on my success and on the recovery of Rashmee both physically and mentally. They, especially the bunch of Sai devotees, attributed all this to the grace of Sri Sathya Sai Baba.

In the meanwhile, my wife's devotion to the Lord increased a hundredfold and she started attending all *bhajan* sessions held in the houses of Sai devotees in the town and doing service to the poor and destitutes as she had enrolled herself as a volunteer in the ladies wing of the Sri Sathya Sai Sewa Dal. She missed no chance of going over to Patna, Jamshedpur or anywhere else where the conference of the Sewa Dal was held. Dr. Murthy was the State president of the Sri Sathya Sewa Dal Organisation and during those days much meaningful work was being done in Bihar.

We used to have *darshan* of Sri Sathya Sai Baba periodically in our dreams, not to speak of his imperceptible symbolic presence in moments of need. I remember specially one event that might have cost Rashmee her very life. She used to take a few doses of Largactil-25 mgm. at night to induce sleep. One evening, when she had a row with her mother, she took out a whole strip of Largactil, containing ten tablets, and swallowed the whole lot. When I returned from the university, my wife reported the matter to me. I became nervous and was at a loss to understand what to do. I stood with folded hands before a large picture of Sri Sathya Sai Baba, that was hanging on the wall. The picture started swinging to and fro in spite of the fact that there was no gush of wind. I was unable to make out what this swinging of the picture actually meant. 'Was it a good or bad omen?' I could only make a guess that it must have a salutary and beneficial message since Baba had the infinite capacity to do good to his devotee. Although a controversy raged in the country, specially in the rationalists' quarters about the miracles performed by him, it had hardly any effect on the devotees or on the vast majority of the people who believed in the divinity of Sri Sathya Sai Baba, not only in this country but also in the farthest corners of the globe. From my own authentic experiences and the tokens and emblems of his love, I was more than convinced of the Godlike powers of Sri Sathya Sai Baba. So, I equated the violent swinging of the picture frame in the still and airless room as yet another demonstration of Baba. However, I called for a cab and took Rashmee at once to the out-patients' section of the local Medical College hospital. The medical consultant on emergency duty was acquainted with me. He checked the heart, respiration and pulse rate of the patient and said, 'She is quite all right. Are you sure she had swallowed the pills? I can't believe it as there is no effect on her,' the consultant said firmly.

'I am really surprised. I did not actually see her swallowing the pills. I was told by my wife who must have seen her taking the pills. I saw the torn pieces of the strip of paper in which the pills were wrapped originally,' I said.

'Be that as it may, it is immaterial now. She may have gulped the depressant drug and the poison without being affected by it. This sounds incredible. I do not need to give any antidote. Take her home, sir, and only take care that she does not sleep,' the consultant said.

'Glory be to God!' I whispered in deep gratitude. This was yet another hint, the meaning of which I could only half-guess. But all this confirmed my belief in the divinity of Lord Sai and in his explicit declaration that he was the one God who had incarnated on earth to spread His message of love. I remembered the prophetic announcement of Lord Krishna, while he admonished Arjuna in the battlefield of Kurukshetra that whenever there is a decline of *dharma* and eclipse of the moral and spiritual values and Bharat is engulfed in crisis, he incarnates from age to age.

My wife and I felt a strong and compulsive urge to journey
to Prasanthi Nilayam to witness the radiant sun there and
bask in the glory of Puttaparthi and also to test the veracity of
these hints and guesses. But the journey to Puttaparthi was
something easier said than done. A myth is current that no one
could go over to Prasanthi Nilayam by his own sweet will. One
can go to that hallowed celestial city if only Swami has willed
it. In fact, he was sending summons and signals all over the
world, the signal of love, to all those who were destined to see
him in person. But so great was our impulse and craving to
have his *darshan* that we put it as the first agenda during our
morning and evening prayers. And I must say that our wish
materialised very soon and the boon was granted, to our great
satisfaction. Doesn't God listen to the sincere and ardent
prayers of His devotees?

A fairly senior lecturer of English at the local Woman's
College had submitted her doctoral thesis on Wallace Stevens,
the great modern American poet, under my direction. I had
put two eminent Professors of Mysore and Madras
Universities on the panel of her examiners. They had given the
thesis their approval but had shown their inability to visit
Muzaffarpur to conduct the oral examination of the candidate.
Instead, they suggested that Mysore be the venue of the *viva
voce* test and asked me to undertake the journey to Mysore
along with the candidate. As the summer vacation was on, the
Vice-Chancellor of Bihar University allowed me to proceed to
Mysore for this important official work and granted the usual
travelling and daily allowances for the purpose. The candidate
was informed of the date and venue of the test and she was
only too happy to go to Mysore along with her husband so that
she could combine pleasure with profit. It was really a strange
coincidence and I was inclined to think that some mysterious
force had made this beautiful arrangement to enable us to go
over to the land of our heart's desire.

The stage was set for the fateful journey, and there was no
stopping our enthusiasm. My wife looked very quiet and
serene and the sublime feelings of devotion and ecstasy
reflected on her countenance. As for Rashmee, she was excited
about the prospect of a long journey to South India. Like
Richard Crashaw, I was fired by a desire to reach that radiant

zone of light and be face to face with the Lord:

> Much less mean we to trace
> The Fortune of inferior gemmes,
> Preferr'd to some proud face
> Or perch't upon fear'd diadems.
> Crown'd Heads are toyes. We go to meet
> A worthy object, our Lord's feet.
>
> Richard Crashaw, *Saint Mary Magdalene*

We reached Howrah station where we were supposed to change the train on time. We had our reservation in the express train leaving for Madras in the evening. As a strike was going on in the Railways, the train was cancelled. We were quite upset as we had to make sure that we reached Mysore well before the date for the *viva voce* test of the candidate. I met the official in-charge of reservations and requested him to arrange sleeping berths in the next train, the Howrah-Madras mail. The official was very helpful and obliging and he made provision for three sleeping berths and a couple of seats. So, we travelled up to Madras in a fairly comfortable manner. The journey from Madras to Bangalore was smooth and easy on a fast express train and we reached Mysore well in time for the oral test of the candidate. The Professor of English, who happened to be one of the most brilliant English Professors in the country, invited us to lunch at his residence after the completion of the test and we enjoyed our stay in Mysore as we took time out to visit the famous Brindavan Gardens. Next morning we undertook the return journey to Bangalore and boarded the train going to Dharmavaram. We reached Prasanthi Nilayam round about noon. By some queer and strange logic, the candidate, Mrs. Prasad, who should have been rejoicing at the acquisition of her Ph.D. degree, could not withstand the strain of the journey; the South Indian food did not suit her at all and she was taken ill. She and her husband parted from us on reaching Prasanthi Nilayam and took lodgings in a hotel in front of the gate of the *ashram*. We went to the accommodation office of the *ashram* and a room in the East Prasanthi Block was allotted to us. Since there was still an hour left for the *darshan* of Sri Sathya Sai Baba in the afternoon we hurriedly changed our clothes, had lunch at the *ashram* canteen and proceeded towards the temple.

Devotees were thronging in a lawn outside the temple so
that they could get their assigned places in the different rows
in the *darshan* line. Everyone wanted to get a seat in the first
line so that a close view of Swami, the touching of his lotus feet
or conversation with him could be assured. So, lots were
drawn. Later I came to realise that it all depended on the sweet
will of Swami. In case he wished to grant an interview to a
devotee, he called him even from the last row in the assembly.
But such is human curiosity and compulsion that people
waited endlessly for a chance of getting a seat in the first row.
Since there was separate space in the lawn for male and
female devotees, my wife and Rashmee occupied their seats in
the female section. They were fortunate to get the first row in
the line. I occupied my seat in the male section and waited for
the appearance of Swami, as everyone else did.

Swami, emerged from the temple in his familiar red robe
and stepped out slowly to the open field. His movement
appeared to me to be supple and rhythmic. There was a hush
all over the place and all eyes were fixed on the face of Baba
and on the coronet of his black and velvety hair, resembling
the locks of Lord Shiva. The face shone with the light of a
thousand suns, as it were, at that time. The sun slanted
westward and the imperial star sent its rosy beams down to
the hallowed spot, turning the whole scene crimson. It was a
scene out of a dream territory. The figure of the greatest saint
and God man of India, who had the largest following in the
world, not only in India, but also in the remote corners of the
continents, moved slowly on the sandy tract, and cast his eyes
all round. Indeed it was a memorable scene, destined to remain
etched in my memory for ever. It was not just a common sight,
but a scenario bathed and drenched in love:

> The hour of sight,
> Flower of light
> And unendurable
> Wings of flight.
> The play of light
> In the wake of the sun
> Is suddenly still
> Like a frozen stream.

Suddenly still
Bird, flower and shell
That love has created
Life-shaped and perfected,
So to remain.
                         Kathleen Raine, *Still Life*

He waved his hand in the air and materialised the sacred
vibhuti and gave it to some of the devotees. I noticed Sri
Sathya Sai Baba gliding gently like a swan in a placid lake. He
stopped at the place where my wife and daughter were sitting
in the first line. He allowed them to kneel at his lotus feet and
with a gesture of his hand pointed towards the small corner of
the verandah in the mandir. My wife, followed by my
daughter, walked towards the right corner of the verandah.
Dr. Murthy, the State president of the Sewa Dal Organisation,
Bihar, who happened to be sitting behind me, asked me to go
and wait in the front verandah. 'If the female member of a
family is picked up for personal interview, the male member
and the head of the family is also entitled to go,' he added.
'How fortunate! You just arrived an hour ago and Swami has
chosen you and your family for interview.' I walked up to the
verandah, in an ethereal mood. It was good to think that my
plaint was heard and that I would soon be standing face to face
with the Lord. And I fervently believed that it would herald a
new season of faith and hope and love that would mark the
beginning of my blessedness and the end of all my sorrows!

From the verandah I saw the figure in red apparel going
round the semi-circle formed by the assembled audience, and
picking up a few more persons for interview. After ten minutes
or so, Sri Sathya Sai Baba, loving and reverentially called
'Swami' by the Ashramites and general run of people at
Prasanthi Nilayam came to the verandah where we exchanged
some words with persons who had the privilege to sit on the
verandah. Finally, he walked briskly to the interview room.
He came out of the room and scanned the faces of all those
whom he had signalled to come for an interview. Coming close
to Rashmee, he asked, 'Where is your papa? Please call him.' I
moved forward and stood near Baba. He looked into my eyes
and there was such transparency in those beautiful eyes as I
had never seen before in any human eye. I had forgotten at

that moment that I was actually standing near God, who, according to his own declaration made in Bombay was the incarnation of God in human form, whose mystery and magnificence the entire humanity, even if engaged perennially in trying to get at his reality until millennium, would not be able to understand. As I recollected every phrase of his announcement recorded in so many authentic books on Sri Sathya Sai Baba, I was overwhelmed with a deep sense of awe. The beautiful lines of the seventeenth century religious poet, Henry Vaughan, flashed on the screen of my mind:

> There is in God (Some say)
> A deep but sizzling darkness; As men here
> Say it is late and dusky, because they
> See not clear;
> O for that night! Where I in him
> Might live invisible and dim.

Henry Vaughan, Night

There was a luminous halo on his face and radiant beams of love fell on us and everywhere. Sri Sathya Sai Baba took a few paces towards me and placing his right arm over my shoulders, said warmly in a very soft accent, 'Come into the room.' We entered the small corner room and he followed us. We knelt at the lotus feet and waited. Then he took us to another room adjacent to that room. It looked like an attic room just below the stairs going up to the first floor, Swami stood so close to us that we were bathed in the aroma of his presence. It was the same kind of perfume that we smelt in our shrine at Muzaffarpur. Baba looked at Rashmee tenderly and, turning towards me, he said most affectionately in monosyllables, 'She has a mental weakness. I know all about your sufferings and troubles.'

Tears surged into my eyes to hear his tender and affectionate words and the waves of oceanless love surging from his divine eyes seemed to envelop and sway my whole being.

'That's why I have come to you, Swami, for mercy and succour,' I murmured in a rasping tone.

He whispered gently, 'Do not worry. Swami will set everything right.'

Then he circled his right hand in the vacant space and a palm full of *vibhuti* appeared instantly which he gave to each of us and said, 'Do eat it,' he added. 'She will be all right gradually if she takes *vibhuti* regularly for some time. I shall be giving some more *vibhuti*.' He took out small packets of *vibhuti* from a basket and gave a handful to each of us.

'Swami, shall we give her the tranquillizers as well?' I asked.

'You may not. That will not be necessary,' he said.

We once again touched the lotus feet and, filled with a deep sense of gratitude, walked out of the room.

As we came out of the room and proceeded towards the *ashram* canteen for the purpose of taking some evening tea and snacks, many devotees accosted us on the way and made eager inquiries out of sheer curiosity. 'What transpired at the interview?' asked Dr. Murthy, the State president of Sai Dal Organisation, who lived at Jamshedpur.

Since it was a purely personal affair, I just gave a general reply, 'Oh, it was wonderful. Swami is all-knowing and he is truly a fountain of love.'

'You are telling me!' exclaimed Dr. Murthy. During the evening *bhajans*, we sat in the temple hall and had the occasion to see Swami seated on the dais moving his hands in a rhythmic gesture in tune with the *bhajan*. Then he withdrew for a while, only to appear again during *arati*. We took our dinner in the canteen and retired to our room in East Prasanthi. My wife was beaming with joy as she had got a number of occasions to touch the lotus feet of the Lord. Since the lady lecturer from Muzaffarpur and her husband were not to be seen anywhere during the *darshan* time or during the *bhajan* I was worried about her. But I was so happy about our experience of the first day of our visit to the celestial city that I cast all other thoughts away.

'I do not see Mrs. Prasad. Where has she gone? I suppose she has gone to Bangalore,' said my wife.

'Maybe. She was unwell in the morning on alighting from the bus. You know, everyone has his or her own *karma*, let us take a good night's rest. Tomorrow morning after the *darshan* of Swami, we shall proceed to Bangalore en route to Madras and Muzaffarpur,' I said to my wife.

'Oh, what a dismal prospect. I like this place very much because here is paradise and the very Lord of the universe lives here.'

I remembered the line of an English *bhajan* sung by some American devotees on a long playing record which I had heard. 'Who is Sai Baba? He is love, love, love', and its companion piece:

'Sai Baba... Sohum... You and I are one.'

On that night, I had a sound sleep and had recurrent dreams of the portals of heaven, angels and choirs. Waking up at the twilight hour of dawn, we prepared ourselves for joining the *prabhat pheri*, the row of men and women walking around the premises of the *mandir*, chanting *bhajans*. Soon afterwards, the business of the day began, crowds assembled in front of the statue of Lord Ganesha. Devotees thronged the milk booth and vegetable shop located in the *ashram*. As I was going towards the canteen for tea, I met one whom I was very pleased to meet. He was none other than my generous and warm-hearted friend and benefactor, Professor Vinayak Krishna Gokak, the most illustrious figure in the discipline of English literature in the country, a great Kannada poet and an arch devotee of Sri Aurobindo and Sri Sathya Sai Baba. I had seen him last at Shimla while I was working there as a Visiting Fellow and he was the Director of the All India Institute of Advanced Study. He was visibly surprised to see me.

'You here?' he enquired. 'How is your daughter now? I could not see you when you suddenly left Shimla. I was away in New Delhi and came to know about the circumstances under which you had to resign and go back to Bihar. I felt very sad about it. I know how you must be feeling. I have had a similar and identical affliction and destiny. My daughter, you know, had a chronic mental weakness and she had to be kept in chains. Once while I was away to the UK to deliver a lecture on Indian English Literature at the University of Leeds, she remained in Bangalore under the supervision of her mother. Just at the time when I was going to deliver my talk at the University in Leeds, I received a cable informing me that my daughter had ended her life by her own hands. She had flung herself into the well in my compound. You can imagine how desolate and miserable I felt. But duty had to be done. So I

went to deliver my lecture in spite of the personal tragedy that
was so finely wrought in my life by some invisible force. But I
am happy you have come to the right place now. In a case like
this, all you can do is to evoke the blessings of God or get rid of
your darling for ever by sending her to an asylum for life. Too
much of love is a destructive element, anyway. I mean human
love. But as I said, Divine Grace, or even a fragment of it, can
work miracles and redeem human suffering,' Professor Gokak
said under the stress of personal feeling and the sad memory of
the loss of his daughter.

'Swami blessed her only last evening. He assured me that
the patient would recover in good time,' I said.

'I am delighted to hear it. I have been living under the
shadow of the Lord, and I know that he is infinitely kind and
compassionate as only God can be. Now you can rest assured.
Your problem will be solved,' Professor Gokak said warmly.

I took leave of Professor Gokak and watched his tall and
robust figure moving towards the *mandir*. I was aware of the
fact that Professor Gokak, like some very distinguished
personalities of India and the world, was a devotee of Sri
Sathya Sai Baba and that he was the educational adviser to
him and subsequently had taken over as the founder Vice-
Chancellor of the prestigious Sri Sathya Sai Institute of
Higher Learning, a deemed university. I also had the privilege
of reading his book, *Sri Sathya Sai Baba: Man and Avatar*.

After the morning *darshan* we had our breakfast at the
canteen and visited the bookstall where I purchased a number
of books on Sri Sathya Sai Baba. As we came out of the *ashram*
bookstore, I stumbled into another very important personality
of the *ashram*. He was Dr. Bhagwantham, formerly adviser to
the Ministry of Defence, Government of India. I greeted him
and introduced myself and spoke to him about my personal
predicament and interview with Baba. I found that he was a
firm believer in the divinity of Baba and said confidently, 'He is
certainly an Incarnation of the Lord. I have absolutely no
doubt about it. Keep on worshipping him, and you will be
rewarded,' Dr. Bhagwantham said.

My wife went around the shops outside the *ashram* and
bought photographs, rings and curios for distribution to
friends and relatives back home. The morning sun was

ascending higher up in the sky and the sound of the *bhajan*
reverberated in the air. Descending the stairs, we came to the
ground floor and casting a wistful look at the temple we found
Sri Sathya Sai Baba moving in the field full of devotees who
were chanting the lines of the *bhajan* in chorus. It was a
singular good fortune to get a glimpse of the Lord at the time of
leaving the *ashram*. My wife, who looked particularly sad,
remarked, 'I wish we had stayed here for a couple of days
more. We have not even seen the notable spots like the
Chitrawati river, the *Kalpataru* tree on the hillock and the
house in the Puttaparthi village where Baba was born. To
come all the way to this abode of peace and heaven of bliss and
to go back without seeing those places?... It is really very
depressing. Isn't it?'

'Mother, please don't sulk. You had the good fortune of a
personal interview with Swami on first ever visit to Prasanthi
Nilayam. People come here time and again...a thousand times
from far-away corners of the globe and yet fail to get the grace
of Swami. Really mother, you have the habit of complaining,'
Rashmee said.

'Yes, Rashmee is right. Think of our good fortune. We are
not returning empty-handed. We have received Swami's
blessings and shall be coming here again and again so long as
we live. Let us merge ourselves into the divine and cultivate
nearness with Swami in our heart and soul. The rest is not our
business. Love, ardour, selflessness and self-surrender are the
virtues we need to foster within ourselves. So, cheer up. If
things are favourable, we might think of coming here again
next November to attend the birthday function of the Lord,' I
assured her.

The bus of the Karnataka State Transport Corporation,
took us away from the land of our heart's desire and I was
transported in my imagination to another place, another
time... to Little Gidding, a small place in Huntingdonshire,
England. The lines of T.S. Eliot's timeless poem summed up
my aspirations:

> If you came this way,
> Taking any route, starting from anywhere,
> At any time or any season,
> It would always be the same. You would have to put off

Sense and notion. You are not here to verify,
Instruct yourself or inform curiosity
Or carry report. You are here to kneel
Where prayer has been valid. And prayer is more
Than an order of words, the conscious occupation
Of the praying mind, or the sound of the voice praying.
                  T.S. Eliot, *Four Quartets*, Little Gidding, i, 39-48

We boarded the bus going to Dharmavaram and got the
train connection to Bangalore. All along the way, my mind was
set on heavenly things. I marvelled at the supreme and
ineffable peace that prevailed at Prasanthi Nilayam and at the
glory of Sri Sathya Sai Baba. However, I must say that I was
still a doubting Thomas, for my rational thinking and scientific
temper made me rather sceptical at times. I had read a lot
about the theory and concept of incarnation in the scriptures,
about the Greek Logos, the Word in Christian theology and the
idea of the Supreme Brahman in Indian mythology. The
Supreme Power who had created the universe and the cosmos
incarnated in the created universe, from time to time to reveal
his glory and power and to teach mankind by both precept and
example the righteous path and this gospel of love. Whenever
humanity strayed from the straight path of moral
righteousness or *dharma* the Lord appeared in human form.
Apart from the major *avatars* who have directed and shaped
the course of history and are worshipped by human beings,
there have been a number of prophets and saints and seers
who have taken birth on this planet to teach mankind the
lesson of love and principles of practical day-to-day ethics.
There have been complete *avatars* like Krishna and a host of
lesser *avatars*, prophets and seers. But, still mankind is not
blessed, it is only to be blessed.

In the modern age which is verily an age of anxiety and
total eclipse of faith, man stands at the threshold of
annihilation. And the advent of the Lord had been imperative.
Hence, the declaration of Sri Sathya Sai Baba that his advent
at the present phase of crisis was to save mankind from
imminent catastrophe and destruction seems to be timely and
propitious. Sri Sathya Sai Baba has cautioned people against
blind faith or acceptance of his words without testing them or
verification. Nor does he ask devotees to change their mode of

worship of their chosen God. All he wants is the crystalline purity of the heart, lucid transparency of thought and offerings of love. At the same time, he says, 'Come and see for yourself, test my reality from your personal experience.' However, he also hints that with limited and finite human perceptions, it may be well-nigh impossible to grasp the quintessential reality of the Divine.

From my own personal experiences of which I have given a fairly comprehensive account in the preceding chapters, I can say that the light of the blazing sun has scattered much of the darkness of my life and has removed the darkness of life, the agony and the torment of existential encounters.

I feel from a purely personal, visionary and poetic perspective that an *avatar* does not need to kill demons or destroy the evil symbolised by monsters, any longer. He has to correct the *buddhi* or intelligence of mankind and bring out an utter transformation in him. I believe in the significance and meaning of the hints and indications which are emblems of love and stand inevitably for Incarnation. It is only through these hints during the moments of visionary gleaming that one has the sudden illumination and is able to comprehend the reality of God and one experiences a lifetime's death in love. The question that amazed me most was that Sri Sathya Sai Baba had wrought a transformation in my thought and feeling. I had learnt to shed my ego and to practise the virtue of humility. And my spirit was no longer exasperated or tainted by rage or fright. And the love of Swami and his tender concern for the well-being of my daughter had transubstantiated all. I resumed my duties at the university with a newly gained poise and serenity and liked to think that I was no more than an instrument in the hands of God for rendering some service to humanity.

I found myself in much calmer waters now and resumed my creative writing with great zeal and concentration. It was an exercise and a discipline which I could not have resorted to during those calamitous years of disaffection and dejection. My present state of mind was very much like that of the seventeenth century religious poet, George Herbert:

And now in age I bud again,
After so many deaths I live and write:
I once more smell the dew and rain,
And relish versing...

George Herbert, *The Flower*, 36-38

At that time I was all too conscious of the contrastive phases of the past gloom and present felicity. I completed writing two novels in Hindi and derived the maximum amount of artistic pleasure. At the same time, I discharged my functions in the Department of English to the best of my abilities and was by and large, successful in placing the Department on the all-India map. The sky was the very limit of my aspirations and achievements. I organised a national seminar on Confessional Poetry in which some eminent Indian and American Professors participated and read their papers. On that occasion, I invited the distinguished guests to the Wednesday *bhajan* session which used to be held at my residence. After the *bhajan* came to a close and *prasad* was distributed, Rashmee gave a demonstration of her artistic talent by performing a monoact on a devotional theme related to Sri Sathya Sai Baba. A middle-aged lady in a torn white sari, her hair all dishevelled, was spotted in a corner of the hall. She refused to take the sacred ashes or the plate containing the *prasad*. She asked Rashmee to show her the way out of the hall. As we were all busy attending to the distinguished guests who seemed to be visibly impressed by the quality and timbre of the beautiful Sai *bhajans*, Rashmee came running from outside the hall and exclaimed in a voice charged with surprise, awe and disbelief. 'Papa, Papa... that woman...'

'What about that woman? Did you offer her the *prasad*? She looked as though she had lost her wits. Poor, crazy woman,' I said.

'That woman was an elf... an airy insubstantial thing...' Rashmee fumbled. 'It's simply unbelievable.'

'What do you mean?' I queried.

'When I offered her the plate of *prasad,* she refused it and said, "Show me the way out of here... I should be going now..." She followed me down the garden alley, stepped out on the street and sailed ahead in the deepening dusk... and lo and

behold, she melted into thin air and disappeared. Papa, I just
can't believe it. I doubted if I was waking or asleep. She must
be a ghost,' Rashmee said thoughtfully.

Sri S.P. Atri, the gentle and pure-hearted devotee of Baba,
who was present by my side, said at once, 'Neither a ghost nor
a goblin... She must be Baba, assuming another form... It is
customary for him to appear in a different guise at the houses
of his close devotees. Glory be to the Lord!' Mr. Atri's voice was
impassioned and he folded his palms in gesture of *vandana*.

On that night, the quantity of *vibhuti* and *kumkum*
appearing on the pictures and the floor was profuse and the
whole room smelt of the familiar aroma permeating the air at
Prasanthi Nilayam. Rashmee kept on making steady progress
on the road to normalcy. My wife's joys new no bounds and our
faith in the Godlike attributes of Sri Sathya Sai Baba deepened
further. As a sequel to all these happy events, and the season
of rejoicing, there was another event in the offing, the wedding
of my son with a girl of his choice. And indeed life seemed to be
glorious!

The happy event, performed in the spring, marked the
advent of peace and felicity in the family. My wife, who
thought continually of Swami, suggested that we should pay a
visit to Prasanthi Nilayam with the newly married couple for
Baba's blessing on them. Not only my wife, but also I had
developed a mind-set to think of the Lord all the time and to
surrender all actions and thoughts to the very source, and to
believe that it was the will of Baba that prevailed. And we had
learnt the lesson that all our joys and griefs were offerings to
God:

> Teach me my God and king,
> In all things thee to see
> And what I do is anything,
> To do it for thee.
>
> George Herbert, *The Elixir*, Stanza 1

Indeed, the relationship of man and nature, and every
event in the phenomenal world, with the Eternal becomes
explicit the moment one senses the grandeur of God:

And for all this, nature is never spent;
There lives the dearest freshness deep down things;
...The Holy Ghost over
World broods with warm breasts and with 'bright wings'.
                    G.M. Jopkins, *God's Grandeur*

As the summer vacation was only a week ahead and both
my son and daughter-in-law were presently in town, we
decided to leave for Prasanthi Nilayam. I booked the train
reservation ten days in advance of the stipulated date of the
proposed journey. While my son was very enthusiastic about
the trip, unexpected and stubborn resistance came from my
daughter-in-law. However, after a great deal of persuasion,
she consented to go on the condition that she should be allowed
to go to her father's place as she intended to make certain
applications for the post of a lecturer in a couple of Women's
Colleges in the university. My wife offered to accompany her to
the city and bring her back a day before the scheduled date of
departure. But, unfortunately, my daughter-in-law did not
keep her word and my wife returned, weary and crestfallen
one burning summer afternoon. She looked visibly upset.

'Is there anything the matter with you? You are so gloomy
and upset,' I asked her with apparent concern.

'Do not ask me, she never meant to go to Prasanthi
Nilayam. It was just a ruse. She is so absolutely self-willed and
stubborn. And the way she treated me! I was staying with my
brother in the city and sent a messenger to her asking her to
get ready for the journey back to Muzaffarpur. She sent a note
saying that she was unwell and that her parents have advised
her not to undertake the strenuous journey down south. So, I
felt thoroughly disgusted and disappointed. What pains me
most is that our desire to go to Prasanthi Nilayam has been
thwarted. What would Swami think of us?' my wife said
ruefully.

'Do not grieve. Take it to be the Divine dispensation. You
know, not even a leaf shakes without his assent, but don't
worry. We shall surely go to Prasanthi Nilayam at a more
auspicious time... the birthday festival in November. As for our
daughter-in-law, you should not feel uneasy or sad. She's
attached to her parents and we are, as yet, complete strangers

to her. Besides, she does not know much about Baba at this stage,' I tried to console her.

Rashmee was particularly unhappy, for she loved travelling and going over to Prasanthi Nilayam pleased her most. She naturally sulked and even cursed her sister-in-law for backing out. However, my son remained quite unconcerned. He decided to go over to Calcutta to work at the National Library.

Rashmee sulked for a couple of days, but she was satisfied when I offered to take her to Varanasi where I had to attend a meeting of the Board of Courses of Studies in English at the Benares Hindu University. She enjoyed the trip and went about seeing the famed historical place, temples and monuments. But for me, the summer had turned out to be a summer of discontent. I still waited for more indications so as to bring cheer to my drooping spirits. I still hankered for those hints which symbolise the higher levels of mystical experience and divine grace. Still in the process of emerging from the terrible catastrophe of the past pain and experiencing the dark night of the soul, I cried, like G.M. Hopkins:

No worst, there is none, pitched past pitch of grief,
More pangs will, schooled at forepangs, wider wring,
Comforter, where, where is your comforting
Mary, mother of us, where is your relief?
                    G.M. Hopkins, *No Worst, There is None*

The strange, unseemly behaviour of my son's bride had set me thinking about the future. She did not seem to be gentle or considerate and so I wondered if she was the girl who could give emotional stability to my son. However, there was no use thinking of what had been and what might be in the future. I decided to leave everything to God to make or mar the fortunes of my dear children.

I experienced a sense of disaffection. The only way I could get over this feeling was to immerse myself wholeheartedly into my creative writing. I wrote a couple of short stories and transcreated them into English. The writing relieved the tension within me to a large extent. And the unrest slowly and gradually subsided when I engaged myself in the patterns of meditation on the absolute sole lord of the universe, expecting to receive the token of his grace.

All through the *bhajan* sessions on Wednesdays and continual service to the poor and the destitute, my wife attuned herself to the divine with her whole soul alive. The Sai devotees of the town admired her wholesale consecration to Sri Sathya Sai Baba and took lessons from her example. She was given charge of the female section of the Sri Sathya Sai Samiti and was even sent for training to Jamshedpur as a Bal Vikas teacher. Her devotion to Baba had truly reached its zenith and it appeared to me that her face shone with the effulgence of God's love. She had found a purpose in her life. Having been purified in the flames of suffering and pain, she had been transformed into pure gold. Everything else had become secondary to her in her constant pursuit of *aradhana* and *bhakti* of Sri Sathya Sai Baba whom she had fully accepted as her *guru*. Her whole being seemed to be aflame with the glow of sublime and deathless devotion and her eyes were lit up with a strange ardour. I could very well understand her feeling of discontent and despair on being deprived of the chance of going over to Prasanthi Nilayam. I tried to assuage her feelings and assured her that we would surely make it in November when a mid-winter spring generated the heart's heat and brought fluorescence to the flowers. She felt more or less comforted and resumed her usual service as the Convener of the Mahila wing of the local Sathya Sai Organisation. She was soon in the realm of enchantment. In a way, the divine discontent had nurtured the life of the significant soil. She had a series of dreams and visions—hints and guesses at regular intervals. We had placed a beautiful table lamp in the shrine. The light came on by itself everywhere and footprints in *kumkum* and *vibhuti* appeared on the floor which were collected and stored in separate containers.

One day a young lad from Barauni came to see us. He introduced himself as a devotee of Baba. He told us that he had had a fall while playing football and had visited Puttaparthi to seek Swami's blessings and grace so that he could get relief from constant pain in the leg. Swami had given him the sacred ashes while he was sitting in the *darshan* line. Back home, he had a marked improvement, but there has been a recurrence of pain, of late. Hearing about the miracles at our place, he had come to Muzaffarpur and was allowed admittance into our worship-room. He scribbled a note addressed to Swami and prayed for *vibhuti*. He shut his eyes and waited. When he opened his eyes, he was delighted to see a substantial quantity of *vibhuti* on the paper. I was in my study when he came running to me, his face beaming with joy. 'Sir, Swami has listened to my plaint. He has blessed me with *vibhuti* and I am sure my pain will subside. How merciful and compassionate the Lord is!' he murmured.

Days and months passed and the summer was over. Rains came and the landscape turned emerald green and pools of water accumulated reflecting the sun-rays in watery mirrors. Then the tidings came from the Convener of the Central Sewa Dal Organisations that before Swami's birthday celebrations, there would be a conference of Sewa Dal volunteers from all over India and that Swami would address the conference. This was indeed a heartening piece of news which gladdened my wife. She planned to avail herself of the opportunity, and for this purpose she introduced three or four other ladies who had enrolled themselves as volunteers only recently. They included Prema, the daughter of Mrs. Sujata, the wife of a Professor of Mathematics at the university, and Mrs. Shanti Chandra, the Vice-Principal of the Mahila Shilpkala School, all of them sincere and keen devotees of Baba. All was set for my wife's much awaited journey to Prasanthi Nilayam. However, I came up against an unexpected obstacle and had to cancel my trip. I was appointed the Dean of Humanities at the university and by virtue of this appointment I became a member of the Examination Board. As the examination for the Master's degree was running behind schedule for the past several years, the Government was keen on seeing to it that the session was regularised. So, the university fixed the date of the examination on the 15th of November and asked me to act as Superintendent of the M.A. examination in Humanities. Thus, the question of getting leave did not arise on account of the emergency. My wife suffered a jolt once again. However, she insisted on going to Prasanthi Nilayam along with other Sai devotees and the three women volunteers. Under this pressure, I had no option but to permit her to go, although I was fairly apprehensive that she might experience unforeseen difficulties as she had never travelled such long distances without a member of the family. But I brushed aside such tears to think that Swami would look after her. In any case I could not think of standing in her way when she was going on a noble mission. Who was I to prevent her? The Lord of the universe had beckoned her in her dreams and she had been receiving hints and guesses all the way through.

However, I spoke to Mrs. Atri and her daughter Prema to take particular care of her. At the time of departure, I accompanied my wife to the railway station in order to see her off. The bunch of male and female devotees was already present on the platform. Soon the train scheduled to leave for Calcutta touched the platform. Since reservation was booked in the second class sleeping coach, they boarded the compartment and occupied their seats. I took my wife aside and gave her a few tips. 'Do take care of your health, and make it a point to write to me as soon as you reach Prasanthi Nilayam. Send a detailed account of the goings on there. I feel disconsolate that I will miss the joy and felicity of participating in the birthday function. But I hope to see everything through your eyes. And, finally, come back positively by the close of the month. I shall miss you greatly.'

'Don't worry. I will return in good time. And please stop worrying about me, Swami will not forsake me in moments of need. I have no problem. I am only concerned about you and Rashmee. You must keep proper vigil and keep her in good humour,' my wife said and joined the women volunteers. The guard blew the whistle and waved the green signal. The train glided away slowly. I watched the faces receding. I knew that the devotees who had embarked were all bound together inextricably in common devotion to Baba, and they seemed to be radiantly happy at the prospect of seeing Baba. And I also thought that those who had left the station would not be the same people as those who would disembark. They were all pulled by the most powerful magnet and were sure to be renewed and transfigured by the strange alchemy of divine love.

I returned home and left rather lonely. Rashmee was reading a novel in her bedroom and my orderly was cooking our lunch. And time seemed to have come to a stop. I had never imagined that it would be so difficult to live and work when the

lady of the house was not there. She must be travelling on that
fast express fraternising with the Sai devotees who were so
intimate with her, and singing *bhajans*. And I sat lingering in
the privacy of my residential quarters utterly unable to rid
myself of the human love or *moha*. For a moment, a feeling of
disaffection and disillusion seized my mind.

4
OFT TO A NARROW, HOMELY ROOM

The relationship between the devotee and God is indeed very complex and fascinating. Generally speaking, there are three types of devotees: the seeker, the explorer and the entirely dependent. The first type is motivated by the search for truth, knowledge or *gyan*. He or she wants to see through the veil a glimpse of the Supreme Reality so as to discriminate between appearance and reality. The burden of the quest is verily to get at the centre of things and experience the bliss of enlightenment. The quest for knowledge or enlightenment is a difficult undertaking, costing not less than everything. The ancient *rishis* and *munis* took infinite pains and went through great ordeals involving the mortification of the flesh and abstention from human cravings and desires. They were *sadhakas* in the true sense of the term who made the most stupendous of all bargains and subsequently engaged themselves in ceaseless meditation and *tapasya* in order to envision the Lord:

> Descend lower, descend only
> Into the world of perpetual solitude,
> World not world, but that which is not world,
> Internal darkness, deprivation
> And destitution of all property
> Desiccation of the world of sense
> Evacuation of the world of fancy,
> Inoperancy of the world of spirit;
> This is the one way...
>   T.S. Eliot, *Four Quartets*, Burnt Norton, 114-21

What, for most of us, is difficult or even impossible to attain is absolutely easy, simple and easily achievable for the saint:

> The point of intersection of the timeless
> With time, is an occupation of the saint—
> No occupation either, but something given
> And taken in a lifetime's death in love,
> Ardour and selflessness and self-surrender.
>
> T.S. Eliot, *Four Quartets,* The Dry Salvages, 200-25

Even the heroes in the medieval quest remances were severely tested while undertaking the fateful perilous journey to the chapel where they were supposed to meet the Grail girl and give the right answers to the questions put by her. Only then could they hope to get the mythical Grail and thus complete their quest. In both Hindu and Buddhist thought, the insistence on self-knowledge and *gyan* is recurrent and necessary for the attainment of *nirvana* or liberation. So, the first type of *bhakta* aspires perennially for the highest. God is pleased with the seeker and grants him the boon as in the case of numerous *rishis* and seers and his whole life flowers with divine love, bliss and glory.

The second type of devotee is the explorer, desirous of exploring the *terra incognita,* the mysterious realm of paradise, the shady city of palm trees as described by the Christian mystics. God and all the blessed souls reside in this region in complete harmony and experience the glory of God's love. This type of devotee is fired by zeal and craves for immortality. His reward is consummated love and eternity since he merges his identity with God. His soul, which is a fragment of the divine, finds the ultimate merger or synthesis with the divine. This is the final thrust of the explorer. For the medieval poet, Dante, the exploration maps out the journey through *Inferno, Purgatorio* and *Paradiso* and the different ardours and avenues of the soul until he is face to face with God in the dazzling light of love and sees ingathered all the scattered leaves of the universe, substance and accidents and their relations, as though together fused like a single flame. This ultimate quest is realised at the end of the exploration. But until it is realised, the exploration continues:

> We shall not cease from exploration
> And the end of all our exploring
> Will be to arrive where we started
> And know the place for the first time.
>
> T.S. Eliot, *Four Quartets,* Little Gidding, 240-44

The devotee, when crowned with success in his exploration, acquires the attributes of the divine *Tattvam asi (thou art that).*

The third type of *Bhakta* is entirely dependent on God and surrenders his will to the will of God. This is a condition which is very difficult to attain. The vast majority of humanity turns towards God only when confronted with suffering, sorrow and travail, which is quite fair and natural. Indeed, there is a precious minority that is able to love God for His own sake and develop deathless love and devotion to the Lord. Devotees of such a type, though initially afflicted and tormented by earthly and material problems, learn the value of total surrender to the Lord. Though the *bhakti marg* appears to be apparently simple and easy to cultivate, in reality it is not so. It involves something given and taken, a lifetime's death in love and the highest kind of ardour. The devotion of Saint Teresa to the Christ or of Mirabai to Lord Krishna is entirely an affair of the heart and can scarcely be emulated. But if the devotee has purity of heart and soul and intensity of feeling, and is truly dependent on the Lord, he or she may become one of the chosen few, dear to the Lord. God to such devotees appears to be like father, mother, spouse, friend and all. God does not have His dwelling place in some remote ethereal region of paradise, but in the narrow, homely room of the devotee's heart:

> My dear, dear God! I do not know
> What lodged thee then, nor where, nor how;
> But I am sure, thou dost now come
> Oft to a narrow, homely room,
> Where thou too hast but the least part,
> My God, I mean my sinful heart.
>
> Henry Vaughan, *The Dwelling Place,* 10-16

From my own personal experience I can say that pure, unalloyed, personal love for the Divine is hard to nourish and nurture in the heart contaminated by a thousand and one impurities and gross, wayward impulses. Those who live by the intellect and pride themselves in the resourcefulness and splendour of their minds generally remain at a third remove from divine apprehensions. The simple, naive and unassuming souls or those who have been reduced to a condition of complete simplicity gravitate naturally towards the Divine and are at the receiving end of His redemptive love.

My wife, I should say, without sounding presumptuous or unnecessarily lyrical in her praise, possessed the essential nobility and innate goodness of the soul. The only virtue she hopes to acquire is the virtue of humility. She has in her the compassion and innate sympathy for the infinitely noble, infinitely suffering thing.

She has lived through deep pangs and high agonies, so faith has broken into her life and has transubstantiated all. During my long association with her I have found that she has been truly my better half, having nourished and sustained me and made the maximum amount of sacrifice for the family. No wonder there has been something noble, tender and proud about her personality that speaks for itself at the first meeting. At Muzaffarpur, her total involvement in the work of Sri Sathya Sai Organisations had impressed everyone. Some of the devotees, complete strangers to me, were never tired of speaking highly of her devotion and consecration to the Lord. 'Her life is full of Sai,' they would pronounce. 'Truly she is a *devi*... such a transparent glow and lustre on her face.'

I felt happy that she had gone over to Prasanthi Nilayam and must be feeling radiantly delighted and in her true element up there. And I awaited news from her. I could not stop worrying on her score. 'Would she keep fit there? Who would look after her in moments of need?' These and other such thoughts plagued my mind continually. Although I tried hard to brush such dismal thoughts and forebodings aside, my naked thinking heart made me reflect only on such possibilities. Why shouldn't I leave everything to Swami? Why should I fear when he is here?' My heart's echoes said. But I had lived in the phase of anxiety and grief so long as the concept of simple faith, hope and love always eluded me. I was so greatly possessed of human love that I was not fit for receiving the elixir of God's love. Nor was my heart a suitable abode for the dwelling of the Lord of the universe. But in the case of my wife the chaste cabinet of her heart had become the worthy dwelling place to house the sovereign master of the universe and all created things. This perception proved true time and again. In fact, all the miracles happening in the shrine as well as the numerous hints and gifts were proofs enough, if proofs were needed, of her psychic contact with the Lord.

In spite of all the evidence and testimony, I found, to my dismay, that the doubts lingered in my mind and the clouds of unknowing dimmed my perspectives, faith and belief to a large extent. And I waited fondly for further proofs and clearer, indisputable evidence of the omniscience of God. It was then that I received that wonderful testament from my wife which filled me with ecstasy as it must have touched a sublime and tender chord in the heart of one who had experienced it all.

My wife had given a graphic description of her unique experience at Prasanthi Nilayam which replenished my faith in the divinity of Sri Sathya Sai Baba. Although appearing seemingly incredible and unbelievable, I had absolutely no doubt in my mind that every word of the description must have been wholly authentic, as it was the lived experience of my wife, not just a figment of her imagination. Even the personal interview that Swami had granted to us had shown conclusively that he had the powers that only God can have, the power to know, to console and to cure chronic and incurable diseases. Now it was evident that he had made a permanent dwelling place in the narrow, homely room of my wife's heart and was familiar with even the slightest tremors of her innermost thoughts. I am recording here a few leaves from my wife's intimate journal which is a testament of great significance.

It was a warm and sunny day and the sun was brightest at this time of the year. The entire *Ashram* campus was flooded with light and a soft breeze blew. A large number of devotees squatted in a leisurely fashion on the campus streets and on the streets of the Nilayam. Among the devotees were men,

women from all the corners of the globe, their faces lit up with
animation and expectancy of something auspicious and
beautiful about to happen. They had come all the way from
long distances just for the love of one who had drawn them like
a magnet unto himself and had wrought a transformation in
their lives. No wonder they had come to pay their obeisance to
the Lord who had come to the world to redeem mankind and to
teach the lessons of love, peace, morality and non-violence.
Like everyone else in the jostling crowd I, too, longed to have
the closest view of Baba and to speak to him or be spoken to by
him and to touch his lotus feet. Last evening, I had to sit far
away from him in the last row of the *darshan* line and was
deprived of the chance of speaking to him or touching his feet.
So I was feeling sad and disconsolate and slightly weary and
off colour. The morning *bhajan* was just over and every stall,
bookstall, shop and eating place was full to capacity. I came out
of the *ashram* gate and squatted on the crowded street to have
a look at the picture shops with a view to buying some recent
pictures of Baba. Prema, the daughter of Sri Atri, was with me
and we were talking intimately about our experiences and
comparing notes.

'Didi, tell me, how is Rashmee? I hope she has improved
and leads a normal, meaningful life,' Prema asked me
casually.

'Yes, my dear. She is much better now. Swami had said
that she would improve gradually and would ultimately be all
right,' I whispered.

'What more do you want? You know, the words of Swami
cannot be wrong. Now your problem has been solved. Glory be
to God!' said Prema softly and with immense fervour in her
voice.

'I hope so. But I am concerned about her future,' I said.

'Please do not worry. Swami will surely give her a straight
future. Hasn't the poor girl suffered long enough?' Prema said.

At this moment, there was a commotion on the street and
among the passersby, the red, sleek, imported car of Swami
was seen coming out of the *ashram*—the reason for people
lining up on both sides of the street. The car moved slowly
amidst the assembled devotees and moved in the direction of
Gokulam. The activities on the narrow and congested street

continued as before and we proceeded towards a picture shop, still animated by having a close view of Swami.

'Didi, I have been continually sending my fervent and urgent prayers to Swami for mitigating our griefs and solving our problems. But so far there has been no relief,' Prema spoke in a sad and sombre tone.

'What precisely is your problem, Prema? You have such a nice little compact family and parents, so utterly given to the worship and contemplation of the Lord,' I looked into her eyes.

'That is very true, my dear sister. But you know, the business of living in this world is much more exacting and challenging than you seem to imagine. One must have the wherewithal to subsist. My husband, unfortunately, has been a failure on this front. He is a simple graduate and is not yet settled in life. He cannot hope to get a decent job. My father has been supporting him for so long, but the family is growing and we are in financial straits. I pray to Baba to mitigate our suffering and provide for our *yogakshema* which a devotee has the right to claim,' Prema said ruefully, and a drop of tear like a pearl or a dew drop on a flower bud, appeared in her eyes.

I consoled her. 'Your plaint is bound to be heard and everything will turn out to be fine. All you need is to pray from the bottom of your heart,' I said. 'Baba is very compassionate. He subjects us to rigorous tests and when we are on the verge of a crisis or disaster, he brings about the most welcome and sweet relief.'

'My patience is exhausted and it is proving hard to make both ends meet. Of course, Papa is very considerate and helpful. But I have my own reservations. Besides, my husband has qualms of conscience and hates to be dependent on the bounties of his father-in-law. He is determined to struggle on and fight for economic recovery, but he needs some kind of a break that Baba alone can give him,' Prema said, unfolding her heart.

'Now that you are here, try to speak to Swami on this point. You may even hand over a brief note to him if ever you get a chance to do so before his birthday,' I advised her.

'Look, Swami's car is returning. Let us line up and stand on the pavement,' Prema said.

There was a hush in the atmosphere. People paused, taking a holiday from the busy, barren actions and thoughts, their eyes intent on the car at a distance. The busy, barren life of mend-and-make ceased to matter. The smiling, beautiful face of the Lord seemed to be the only real thing in the vast flux and time-ridden existence of humankind.

Driven by a strange inner impulse, I whispered, 'I wish Swami's car ran me down and trampled me so that every particle of my flesh and bone and each drop of my blood flies to him and scatters over the lotus feet, a real consummation of my desire!'

'What a strange wish! Really, who would not like to have a death so mystical and high!' Prema said, 'but, look, the red car carrying the Lord is speeding so fast, as though it would surmount all barriers!'

'Hush. Let us wait and allow the car to go on by,' I muttered softly. But a strange thing happened. The car came very fast and there was a grating noise of the clutch and the brake. The car stopped just a yard from the place where I was standing. The passersby were all surprised and clustered round the car. Swami opened the door of the car and beckoned me. I drew near him in a nervous and apprehensive frame of mind.

Swami smiled affably and asked, 'Shall I ask the driver to run you over and trample you down so that every portion of your flesh and bone and each drop of your blood flies to me and pours over my feet like a sacred fountain?'

At that moment, there was not a single drachm of blood within me that did not tremble, as I recognised the tokens of divine love. But I hardly had courage enough to look him full in the face or bend down to touch his lotus feet. It was Swami himself who directed me with a gesture of his hand to touch his feet. He was looking at me tenderly as the car moved slowly in the direction of the *ashram* gate.

Many women came rushing towards me and asked all sorts of questions. 'Amma, what did Swami tell you? Why did he stop the car near you? Are you quite familiar with him? It does seem that he is very pleased with you. We have lived at Puttaparthi all our lives, but never before in living memory have we witnessed such a sight... Swami's car stopping on the crowded street and Swami talking to a devotee! Where are you from, Amma? You are indeed very blessed!'

I remained just a mute listener for I was myself overwhelmed by the incident and the superior and special attention given to me by Swami. What was beyond my limited human understanding and comprehension was the fact that Swami had overheard my foolish casual and playful remark voicing my desire to be crushed under the wheels of the speeding car and to be wiped out of mortal existence and be merged with the creator. Prema, too, was rendered speechless and expressed her sense of joy and amazement at my unexpected good fortune.

And she spoke in a soft, sibilant voice, 'Didi, I never imagined even in my dreams that you had drawn Swami so close to yourself by your noble service and sublime devotion. Tell me, how you have done so?'

'I do not myself know, dear Prema. But I have a hunch that it is Swami who has wrought this miracle. Love is no unfamiliar name to me. Swami lives in my heart and this is all I know and need to know!' I mumbled, evading her glance.

I send my greetings to you. Swami's birthday is just a few days away from now. I am keeping very well and am experiencing the greatest sense of rapture. Do not worry. I am well housed and very well looked after. Prema and Sujata are always with me. I will write again after the 23rd November, when I should be able to inform you about the exact date of our departure. I hope Rashmee is well. Thinking continually about Swami and you all.

Yours as ever,
M.

I read the letter several times and the more I read it, the more I was transported to a world of perpetual delight and ecstasy. I felt proud of my wife and admired the depth and intensity of her feeling for Swami that had made her so dear and near to the Lord. As I lay on my bed rapt in pleasant thoughts Rashmee asked, 'You didn't tell me, Papa, what mother had written to you? Is she all right? Has Swami spoken to her?'

'Oh, yes, your mother has been extremely fortunate in this respect. You know how simple and sincere she has been in everything she does,' I said warmly.

'Maybe, you are right, Papa, in your assessment of her nature. But pray, do not be partial towards her. If she has been simple and sincere, I am no less simple and pure-hearted. I love Swami as much. I am the daughter of Swami?'

'Yes, my daughter, you have got a heart of gold and God loves noble and pure souls,' I whispered, trying to put her in good humour. Although she had improved substantially in her mental condition, at times she tended to be provoked by the baser emotions of jealousy, and displayed tantrums of distraction, fits and rage. She was the pale moon which still raged and her rehabilitation could only be possible with divine guidance and help. I fondly hoped that Swami would perhaps intervene at the right moment.

My thoughts were centred on my wife during the next few days and I waited feverishly for tidings from her and her consequent return to Muzaffarpur. But at the same time, I envisioned and contemplated the scenario at Prasanthi Nilayam and imagined the sight of countless devotees sitting in a semi-circle in front of the temple, chanting *bhajans* led by some ecstatic, sonorous and melodious voice. A stanza in Wallace Stevens's celebrated poem, *Sunday Morning,* echoed in my mind:

Supple and turbulent, ring of men
Shall chanting orgy on a summer morn
Their boisterous devotion to the sun,
Not as a god, but as a god might be,
Naked among them like a savage source
Their chant shall be a chant of paradise,
Out of their blood returning to the sky;
And in their chant shall enter, voice by voice,
The windy lake wherein their loved delights,
The trees like seraphim and echoing hills,
That choir among themselves long afterward,
They shall know well the heavenly fellowship
Of men that perish, and of summer morn,
And whence they came and whither they shall go
The dew upon their feet shall manifest.

Wallace Stevens, *Sunday Morning*, Stanza vii

At night when I went to bed and tried to sleep, the images of Prasanthi Nilayam, the domes of the *mandir* and of the beautiful buildings situated on one side of the street, the *ashram* premises and the lovely and the most impressive piece of architecture erected on the top of a hill and the vast open space and the sandy tract of the Chitravati river appeared and reappeared on the screen of my mind. How wonderful it would be if I could take journeys to the hallowed place and spend my life in that heaven, the abode of ineffable peace. Baba appeared in my dream and his *darshan* in the flimsy and insubstantial vague territory of dreams sent waves of delight to me. The next day was a hectic one, as I was supposed to go to the Language Block of the university to supervise and oversee the M.A. examination in Humanities. I asked Rashmee to keep indoors and read novels and magazines or watch television. I also asked the housemaid to be around in case Rashmee needed anything.

My duty as Superintendent of the Examinations proved to be strenuous and pretty tiring. When the day's work was finished and I sent the answer books to the examiners according to the list supplied to me by the university, I returned home. Rashmee opened the door when I pressed the buzzer. She looked very cheerful and greeted me with a smile. 'Look, Papa, the shrine is scented with the fragrant *vibhuti* which is sprinkled all over the place.'

'I will see presently. I am so tired and exhausted. Will you prepare some tea for me?' I said.

'Go and change. I shall be bringing tea within five minutes,' said Rashmee quietly and went downstairs to the kitchen to make tea. I had noticed a welcome change in her attitude to life and things. She loved to be of some service to me and delighted in mixing with people. She was no longer listless, dejected or withdrawn inhabiting her dream world. I remembered the words of Sri Sathya Sai Baba that she would gradually improve and lead a normal life. Tears came into my eyes as I visualised the scene of my first interview with Swami.

While I was sipping the steaming hot tea in the living room Rashmee said with a twinkle in her voice, 'There is yet another piece of good news for you. Mother will be reaching home on the second of December. A telegram arrived in the afternoon. And her letter has also come with today's mail.'

She gave me the telegram and the letter and said, 'I am
going out for an evening stroll and will be back in fifteen
minutes. I will not go very far, just along the campus street.'

'All right,' I said and opened the letter and started reading
it. It was a brief and neat summing up of all that had happened
at Prasanthi Nilayam on the occasion of the birthday festival
which had drawn millions of devotees from near and far. I am
giving here a few excerpts from that letter:

I have related as truthfully as I could the details of my unique
experience which made me feel ecstatic and blessed and
demonstrated most conclusively the omniscience of Baba and
the fact that he permeates our being and dwells in our hearts if
we offer the petals of our love and devotion to him. After
having gone through that crucial and soul-stirring experience,
I was calm and unruffled and realised that serenity and
surrender were all. One has simply to love the Lord and take
both pleasure and pain, joy and sorrow as the *prasad* given to
us by the Lord and that the rest was not our business.

The Bihar contingent of the Sewa Dal volunteers were
assigned work at different points, at the canteen, and at
different gates to control and direct the devotees. I worked in
the canteen, cutting vegetables and during the hour of
darshan I assisted the head volunteer in controlling the
upsurge of the crowd of women devotees who wanted to rush
towards Swami and touch his feet. It was a difficult
assignment inasmuch as the zeal of the devotees could not be
restrained. They broke all the barriers and surged towards
Swami like the surge of waves in the ocean or like a flooded
stream. At times, Swami was so annoyed by their lack of
discipline and decorum that he quit going to the ladies' section.
This was Swami's way of showing his displeasure and it had a
salutary effect on the women. But, given that Prasanthi
Nilayam was flooded with a vast concourse of humanity, and
love was the prime mover at this hallowed place, the crowd
may be said to be, more or less, orderly and disciplined.

The all-India conference of the Sathya Sai Sewa Dal
Organisation got under way in a very impressive manner. The
venue of the conference was the Poorna Chandra Hall. The

hall was full to capacity when Swami gave the divine discourse in Telugu while Professor Nanjundiah rendered it into English. The theme of Swami's discourse centred on the supreme value of selfless service to humanity since *Manav Sewa* was *Madhav Sewa*. Those who spend a lifetime dedicated to the service of the poor and suffering humanity are dear to God and deserve to get both *bhakti* and *mukti*. The assembled audience listened to the speech in silence. So far as I was concerned, the words, images, rhythm and texture of Baba's speech seemed to sink into the central depths of my consciousness. Apart from the wonder-making powers of Baba and his divinity, it was his compassion that touched the tendermost chord in my heart. He had the compassion that characterised the *avatar* and the love that transfigures and transubstantiates all. 'I have come here to foster the devotees,' Baba has declared time and again.

The next morning, all the volunteers were made to sit in a corner in the space in front of the temple and Baba spent a lot of time, speaking individually to the volunteers, offering them uniforms: *dhoti,* sari and scarfs. When he came near me, he cast a loving glance at me and gave me a white silken sari. In the evening Swami gave another discourse on a spiritual theme and at the conclusion of the speech, he sang a few *bhajans.* That was on the eve of his birthday.

On the day of the advent of the Lord, November 23, the sun had arisen crimson clear and bright. Hosts of devotees assembled in front of the *mandir* to see the sun, who came to the terrace of the temple and surveyed the scenario outside. Soon the red car was brought into the field and Swami came downstairs. Sai Gita, the pet elephant, properly decorated, was also at the front of the procession, which moved along the streets of the campus. Prasanthi Nilayam witnessed a sea of humanity. All eating places were full and the shops were doing brisk business. It was nice to see small groups of devotees pouring in from buses and trucks, singing *bhajans.* Their chant reverberated in the air. The quantum of love that the devotees displayed for Sathya Sai Baba was to be seen to be believed. I thought of the people of Ayodhya, Vrindavan and Mathura yearning for the *darshan* of Lord Rama and Krishna, respectively. We love him because he first loved us—that

seemed to be very true in the case of Baba as it had been for
Buddha and Christ. The *avatar* distinguished himself from
other people in one respect: he is the ocean of love and has the
infinite capacity to love. It is indeed love that works out
miracle. One is bathed in the shower of divine love and senses
the glory of the supreme principle of love when one is here at
Prasanthi Nilayam, specially during the greatest of festivals,
the birthday of Baba.

In the evening, there was the central function in the
Poorna Chandra Hall. The chairman of the All India Sathya
Sai Organisation garlanded Sri Sathya Sai Baba, followed by
the presidents of the State Sathya Sai Organisations. But the
most moving and impressive sight was reserved for the close of
the function. Baba, dressed in his white silken robe, his locks
of hair forming a crescent, sat on a swing and as some of his
chosen devotees pushed the swing it began to swing in a
rhythmic fashion. It was indeed a heavenly sight for the
beholder. What gave it its unique grace and resonance was the
bhajan by M.S. Subbalakshmi, the celebrated South Indian
singer, who sang in her sonorous and melodious voice. I had
heard the *bhajans* sung by her in the film *Mira* earlier and
they had haunted me for ever. But the Sai *bhajan* appeared to
be far more haunting and effective as I had the benefit of
seeing the Lord in flesh and blood. To me it seems that the
advantage of worshipping *saguna* Brahma is very great for
one can see and contemplate God in His visual aspect and
image, whereas the worship of *nirakara* Brahma is for the
saints and *rishis* who are already realised souls. The function
continued until midnight and we came out of the hall in a mood
of divine rapture. It was an experience to be treasured in my
memory for all time to come, the last syllable of my conscious
life. Ah, to be in Puttaparthi now when Baba is here! How I
wish you had been here, but I am sure I have given a vivid and
honest account of the festival and you can see the whole thing
from my eyes.

Before I close this letter, let me give another clear and
moving example of Baba's concern for a devotee like me. You
remember I had complained to you about a certain uneasiness
in my left eye? The malady was revived, maybe on account of
loss of sleep, improper rest or infection of some kind. The left

eye turned reddish and got inflamed. I could not withstand the
glare of the sun. My vision was somewhat impaired. What
worried me most was the pain in the eyes. I had gone to the
ashram hospital and consulted the eye specialist. She had
given me an ointment to apply to the eye and told me to foment
the affected eye for relief from pain. She suspected an infection
which had caused conjunctivitis. She had advised me to take
complete rest. However, I could neither foment the eye nor
take adequate rest in view of the busy schedule at the *ashram*.
But Swami knew all.

Once, while I was standing in the field, discharging my
duty as a volunteer, Swami beckoned me with a gesture of his
hand and said, 'Don't stand in the sun. Go and take rest,
otherwise you will hurt your eye.'

'Swami, shall I lose my eyesight?' I mumbled.

'Who says so? It's an infection which will soon be checked.
Go back home after the birthday to your husband. He is
worrying for you,' Swami said, quietly.

'Swami, I pray to you to shape the life of Rashmee, now
that by your grace she is doing fairly well. But her future is
still bleak and uncertain.'

'Do get her married,' Swami whispered faintly and
appeared to be musing over something.

'But her past history... it may be difficult to find a match
for her,' I spoke unconsciously, in spite of myself.

Swami said, 'All you can do is to make an effort and do the
right action. Leave the rest to me.'

I shall discuss this matter in detail. Perhaps the best
course left to us for the rehabilitation of our daughter was to
give her away in marriage to a deserving groom. The rest
depended on her luck and on the grace of God.

In his discourse Swami spoke about the need to cleanse
and purify the sanctuary of our heart, and trim the jungle
of desires and passions. He cited to us the example of
Shabri who had no desire other than the desire to see
Rama and touch his lotus feet and converse with him.
There was no thought in her heart except the thought of
Rama and her life was full of Rama as it were! She waited
in her cottage to welcome Rama. She removed the thorns
and pebbles from the path leading to her cottage and

cleaned it as she cleaned her heart of all the gross and
baser instincts. She tasted each and every fruit which she
had collected for Rama so as to ensure that it was sweet
and fit for the palate of Rama. Shabri was not engaged in
any spiritual exercise. But her heart was full of the
sweetness of Rama's name. She had indeed made her heart
the abode of the Lord and Rama came to her and even
partook of the nourishment in the form of tasted plums.
Baba exhorted the assembled devotees to emulate the
example of Shabri and he assured us that Sai Ram, too,
dwells in the hearts of the devotees if the hearts are as
homely as shrines. He further said that the grace of God
could only be obtained through love, and that love was
divine and it was immortal, everlasting and for ever.
Declaring the purpose of his advent, he said, 'As soon as
the mission is fulfilled, this physical body will not remain.
So, while there is time your only aspiration should be to
offer me the blossoms of your love and the crystalline
purity of your hearts and merge with me as the destiny
and destination of the soul is such a merger with the
divine.' One of my favourite *bhajans* that Swami recited on
the occasion left permanent tremors in the placid and
unruffled surface of my mind and heart. There is nothing
in the world except God. I am closing the letter now. We
are all set for the journey back home. Mr. Atri has gone
over to Dharmavaram to book our train reservation for the
thirtieth of November. As soon as this is confirmed, I will
send you a telegraphic message.

                                                    Yours as ever,
                                                    M.

This letter, like its predecessor, brought a fresh puff of breeze
from the south and set me thinking about my future plans. The
first item on my agenda was the desirability, even the urgency
of altering my perspectives and changing the pattern of my
life. Intellectual exercises and the laws of rational thinking
had failed me in the face of my perilous adventures and
circumstances of my life. I should learn the habit of banishing
self-love and accept every action or fruit of action as
manifestation of divine will and do continual heart-searching.

Like Shabri, I should remove all obstacles and impediments,
every thorn and stone obstructing the passage of the Lord to
the arbours and avenues of my heart. Serenity and surrender
were the only disciplines I need to cultivate and acquire. I
thought about the numerous devotional poets who had given a
voice and a name to their quest for truth and God. I
remembered particularly John Donne's famous sonnet 'Batter
my heart, three person'd God' which seemed to reflect my own
predicament at the moment:

> Batter my heart, three person'd God; for you
> As yet but knocke, breathe, shine, and seeke to mend;
> That I may rise, and stand, O'erthrow mee, and bend
> Your force, to breake, blowe, burn and make me new.
> I, like an usurpt towne, to' another due,
> Labour to admit you, but oh, to no end,
> Reason your viceroy in mee, mee should defend,
> But is captiv'd, and proves weake and untrue,
> Ye dearely' I love you, and would be loved faine,
> But am betroth'd unto your enemie,
> Divorce mee, 'untie, or breake that knot againe,
> Take mee to you, imprison mee, for I
> Except you' enthrall me, never shall be free,
> Nor even chaste, except you ravish mee.
> John Donne, *Batter my heart, three person'd God*

Since I remained in perpetual ambivalence in relation to
God, I often felt uneasy and tormented. However, by nature
and temperament I was sensitive and responsive to the
slightest show of affection and love. But human love possessed
me entirely. I loved my wife and children and felt restless and
tormented if things did not go well with them. If I could love
God with the same intensity, I could make my heart a proper
and fit place for God to reside there. However, I was happy
that my wife, by virtue of her naivete, faith and surrender had
drawn God to herself. I waited anxiously for the time when she
would be back and relate her experience to me. I wanted to
discuss matters concerning the marriage of Rashmee. This
thought had frequently come to my mind ever since her mental
condition showed signs of perceptible improvement. But I was
all too conscious of the hazards involved in the process, firstly,
our family being a distinguished one in the State, was quite

well known. I myself had won a fair amount of recognition and renown by virtue of my intellectual and scholarly pursuit. Those who knew me also knew about my misfortune, specially about the malady that had affected my daughter. So, it seemed to be difficult, if not impossible to find a suitable match for her. Her antecedents and case history could deter anybody from accepting her as a partner for life. Even if some generous or compassionate youth consented to take her as his bride there was no knowing if his parents or the members of his family would let him do so. Besides, Rashmee was not completely cured and I knew that in a disease like chronic schizophrenia, a relapse could not be altogether ruled out. But Swami had advised my wife to make an effort in this direction. The self-same problem of doubt and more doubt, action and inaction, hope and despair gripped my mind. I was aware that the problems of life could not be solved by reason alone or the rational laws of thinking about them. What one is left with is faith and dependence on the divine and confidence in oneself. Perhaps it would be better to take a decision after a frank discussion with my wife and proper resolution of my doubts and dilemma. I must learn to leave everything to the will of God. The impassionate and fervent prayer of Francis Quarles to God rang into my ears:

Thou art the pilgrim's path; the blind man's eye;
The dead man's life, on thee my hopes rely;
If thou remove, I err; I grope; I die.
Disclose thy Sun-beam; close thy wings, and stay:
O thou, that art my light, my Life, my way.
                              Francis Quarles, *Job XII-XXIV*, 43-48

Although I had been blessed with so many hints and guesses and had had fairly insistent intimations of the Lord's grace, I still did not feel the inner compulsion of loving the supreme force that presided over the destiny of all created objects of the world, the compulsion and the pain that prompted Francis Quarles to say 'Thou art my light, my life, my way.'

It was on the second of December that I went along with Rashmee to the railway station to meet the train which was to bring back my wife to Muzaffarpur. The train arrived on time and I spotted my wife alighting from a second class sleeper

coach. She looked rather tired and fatigued. Her left eye was
still inflamed. But her face beamed with joy. We moved down
the platform to receive her. She smiled and turned towards
Rashmee to speak to her. I greeted Mr.Atri and other devotees
who were standing on the platform. They all told me how
fortunate my wife had been to receive special attention from
Baba.

As we came out of the station we talked animatedly about
the function at Prasanthi Nilayam. But my wife was in a hurry
to get back to the university quarters. 'Let's go. We will talk in
detail later. I need rest. My eyes are sore on account of loss of
sleep and the infection,' she said.

'Don't worry. I will take you to an eye surgeon in the
evening,' I whispered.

'I don't think it will be necessary. Swami has given me
vibhuti. I am much better now. Earlier, my eyes were red like
the scarlet *urhul* flower and so swollen that I could not even
open my eyes.'

'There is no question about the cure of conjunctivitis when
Swami is your physician. Still, there is no harm in having a
check-up, if not for anything else then for my personal
satisfaction,' I said tentatively.

'Please yourself and waste money for nothing. I am
familiar with your nature. When will you learn to surrender to
the Lord and silence the phantom of doubts and distractions
arising in your heart?' my wife mumbled in protest.

'You are right, dear. I hide the serpent in the heart that
tempts me to taste the shadow fruit and lose my Eden. And
honestly, I envy you for your complete and unquestioning
surrender to God. Indeed, you are like Shabri and Meera who
made their pure and loving hearts the mansion for the Lord's
permanent residence,' I said, charged with feeling.

Tears rolled down her cheeks and her voice became numb.
She folded her palm and bent her head low as though she saw
the image of the Supreme Being before her mental eye.

'I do not know and I do not understand what good deeds I
have done in my past lives that I have been drawn so close to
the *avatar* and have received a fragment of his blessings. On
that glorious day in Puttaparthi when I expressed my casual
and stray wish to be trampled and crushed under the wheels of

Swami's speeding car, little did I imagine that the Lord resided in the narrow, homely room of my sinful heart and that he knew my innermost thought. I was surprised and overwhelmed when the car actually came to a standstill near me and Swami himself opened the door. "Shall I crush you under the wheels?" he asked, casting a searching glance at me. I was too dumbstruck to tell him that life was burning with a wintry fever and I wanted to merge my being into the divine. And wonder of all wonders was that he was willing to grant my suit and fulfil my wish. Since then my life has not been the same. I have attained the bliss and peace that passeth understanding,' my wife said in a low and sibilant whisper as though she were talking to herself.

'You deserve this felicity, anyway. You have more than your share of suffering. And you know suffering chastens and purifies and transforms the baser metal into pure gold. Besides, love works out the alchemy. All great _bhaktas_, saints and _sadhakas_ die a lifetime's death in love in order to attain oneness with God. Just to give an example, I will tell you about Saint Teresa. The Lord took a private seat, making a mansion in the mild and gentle soul of a soft child. Even at the age of six, she was fired by the love of God and strongly desired to embrace martyrdom to prove how much less strong was death than love. She was destined indeed for a death more mystical and high.' I asked her to listen to a few lines from that poem which would appeal to her very much:

> All those old woes shall now smile on thee,
> And thy pains sit bright on thee.
> All thy sorrows here shall shine,
> All thy sufferings be divine;
> Tears shall take comfort and turn gems,
> And wrongs repent to diadems.
>
> Richard Crashaw, _Hymn to Saint Teresa_, 145-49

I paused and looked at her affectionately.

She blushed and evaded my glance. 'For God's sake, do not raise me to such a pedestal. I am no saint and will need to be born and reborn a hundred times before I become one,' she whispered.

'Work out your own salvation, my dear. You are well and truly on the spiritual path, and Swami will give you _mukti_, I am sure,' I said.

Swami was in our thought continually on that day. Rashmee joined us in the evening and said, 'Papa, promise you will take me to Baba's place next summer. I have to ask him for boons. He cannot be partial towards mother. I am his daughter and he cannot afford to deny me anything.'

'There cannot be any question about it. You better pray to him to give you a husband,' my wife said playfully.

'How shameful! Who cares to get mundane and material things that are so evanescent and ephemeral?' Rashmee muttered.

'What boon would you ask for, then?' I queried, rather amused.

'I would ask for nothing less than love... the love that transfigures and renews,' Rashmee said in an animated voice.

I was fairly impressed and surprised to hear her words. And it struck me that it was the total surrender of her mother to the Lord as well as the love of Rashmee for him that had resulted in her recovery from her dreadful disease. Baba has explicitly declared that the appearance of *vibhuti* on his pictures in your shrine and the sprinking of *kumkum, amrit* and the imprint of his footprints are just his visiting cards, and the miraculous cures of difficult and incurable diseases are manifestations of his love for the patient. If the suffering person or patient loved him with all his soul alive, that love gravitated upwards and ascended to him, and his love, in turn, descended to meet at the intersection point and an immediate and instant cure was the result of the union of two loves. And in this context it seemed to me fairly apparent that Rashmee's cure from schizophrenia was made possible chiefly on account of the essential purity of her heart and the yearning for love and grace. Swami loved and preserved all those infinitely gentle and suffering things who sent waves of love and aspiration towards him. I felt convinced that the redemptive and transfiguring love of God and the healing grace of the Saviour can only be invoked by prayer, discipline and ardour of a rare kind, and the aspirant has to become pure and flawless and make his or her heart the temple for the dwelling of the Lord. Once this is done, the Lord gladly comes down, and settles down in the narrow, homely room of the devotee's heart.

5
TEMPORARY REVERSION: FROM GRIEF TO RELIEF

The central thrust in existential philosophy is obsession with, and a fear of, death and the personal craving for immortality. Thinkers like Saint Augustine, Pascal and Soren Kierkegaard have emphasised the perils of the human condition and the tragic sense of life. As Pascal says, there is nothing more important to man than his own state and he cannot be indifferent to the loss of existence and the perils of everlasting suffering. At the same time, he oscillates between the temporal and the eternal and finds that nothing is more formidable than eternity. The concern with immortality or the paradisal state of beatitude and the need for salvation or *mukti* are the basic tenets of all religions. Emmanuel Mounier believes that everything tells us of the narrowness of life and of the little time for the choice to be made, when contrasted with the immensity of eternity. Since everything tells us of the inevitable finality and immanence of death, it is the solemn duty of man to turn away from the perilous human existence and contemplate the divine. Both in Christian and Hindu philosophy suffering is said to be a catalytic agent that mellows and ripens us and brings us to the promontory from where we can have the vision of what truly matters. It follows from this that enlightenment and self-knowledge come to us the hard way. This journey of life, which in a sense is a pilgrimage from innocence to experience, time to eternity, mortality to immortality, is fraught with unprecedented perils and dangers. There are pleasant arbours, rose gardens, green valleys and lush avenues as well as rocky paths, hilly terrains, thorny paths and precipices and marshy lands where there is no secure foothold. When we reach a milepost we feel happy and contented and voyage forward with hope and joy; when we stumble against dark woods, moss-covered grimpen or mires and fall into yawning abysses, we grieve and curse either God or ourselves. Be that as it may, we rise again and voyage on and stumble and fall again. Thus the journey is a precarious one which can only be completed if one has a clear view of the destination and a firm belief in his purpose and destiny—to reach the city of God and merge his soul into the Infinite. That shady city of palm trees is verily the goal of our pilgrimage and we can reach there only if we have the spiritual resources of hope, faith and love, and do not get swamped by rage and despair if we stumble against odds, landfalls and reversals. If we possess the will and the courage to fare forward and never cease from the fateful quest, the rest will be done by God himself. Henry Vaughan's ardent prayer is wholly relevant in this context:

> O Father of eternal life, and all
> Created glories under thee.
> Resume thy spirit from the world of thrall
> Into true liberty.
> Either disperse these mists. Which blot and fill
> My perspective (still), As they pass,
> Or else remove me hence unto that hill.
> Where I shall need no glass.
>
> Henry Vaughan, *Ascension Hymn*

Since joy and sorrow, pleasure and pain grief and relief, affliction and redemption are very much a part of the existential human condition and form part of the cyclic and recurrent rhythm of existence, I always felt apprehensive about something going amiss in the future. Probably, my past experience of deep and continual suffering and continual affliction had much to do with it. Besides, my faith in God had not crystallised fully enough to be unshakeable and unbreakable. I was all too conscious of my own inadequacies and felt, like George Herbert, that I was not worthy to receive his grace:

But as I can see no merit
Leading to this flavour;
So the way of fit me for it
Is beyond my saviour.
As the reason then is thine;
I disclaim the whole designe;
Sinne disclaims and I resigne.

George Herbert, *Dialogue*

As I was still struggling within myself to perfect my will
with the divine will and taste the bliss that emanates from
total surrender to God, he ordained more misery for me in
order to pull me out of the morass and teach me the holy way.
Contrasted with my predicament of lurking doubt and
waverings and oscillating between faith and scepticism, my
wife led a much more serene and quiet existence. It may not be
wrong to say that she had attained the calm of mind and
complete affirmation of divine love and grace so that no crisis
could ruffle or disturb the poise and serenity of her mind. It is
a truism that humankind cannot bear very much reality
unless fortified by supreme faith and belief in God. So during
the phase of crisis that was in store for us very soon, I was
shocked, mutilated and torn and burnt in the hellish fires of
agony and torment of the deepest magnitude. My wife who was
with me during those calamitous days, remained as serene as
ever and continued to pay her obeisance to the Lord at the
ashram in Brindavan, Whitefield.

In reality, it was the worst kind of reversion that shook the
very fabric of my faith. On account of Rashmee's insistence
and the general wish of her mother and my own wish for a
holiday during the summer, we set out for a trip to Prasanthi
Nilayam with the sole purpose of having a *darshan* of Sri
Sathya Sai Baba. My wife was excited about the prospect of
going once again to the south. We took the express train to
Howrah and changed trains for Madras and Bangalore. We
reached Prasanthi Nilayam early in May when the weather
had turned around with the onset of summer. We had the
greatest disappointment in store for us when a strange kind of
hush pervaded the atmosphere of the *ashram* premises. There
were very few people to be seen in the open space in front of the
mandir and weary, time-ridden faces moved on the streets

along the *ashram* offices and the canteen. We went to the accommodation office and easily got a room in the round building for a couple of days. I asked the person in-charge of the accommodation, 'Everything seems to be unusually quiet. Is Swami not here at the moment?'

'No. He is at Brindavan, Whitefield, and will come here only in June,' the man said, as he turned towards some other visitor.

We moved out and walked wearily towards the round building at the extreme end of the *ashram*. I watched the faces of my wife and daughter which appeared to be sad and crestfallen.

'Papa, why didn't you ask about Swami's whereabouts at the Bangalore station? If you had done so, we would have gone straight to Whitefield instead of coming all the way to Puttaparthi!

'Right, but, don't worry, we shall proceed to Bangalore as soon as we can take a rest for a day or two and freshen up after the strain of the long journey,' I said.

Rashmee looked vacantly at me and said, 'What a shame! We came here all the way in the heat of the Indian summer to see Baba and he is playing hide and seek with us.' She laughed, a quite unnecessary and needless laughter. I noticed a peculiar kind of frenzy in her eyes and the deepening sign of mental emptiness. I also noticed sure signs of paranoia in her eyes and expression. She had set her heart on seeing Baba soon after landing at Puttaparthi. She seemed to have been sorely disappointed and shocked to find out that he was at Whitefield. She kept on pressing me hard to leave for Bangalore without any delay. After a time, it almost became an obsession with her. 'I came here with such great hopes to ask boons from the Lord, but he is hiding at Whitefield. How unlucky I am! He does not love me anymore. Papa, tell me, am I not his daughter? Has he disowned me?' she pestered me with such questions so frequently as to tire my patience. During the night, she kept awake until midnight and exhaled deep sighs of anguish. 'Where are you, Swami? Have you no concern for me and for my feelings? What shall I do to the demon who threatens me with his terrible face and grimace? How can I make good my escape from the clutches of the

dragon? Save me, O Lord, save me from the dragon! You... who
are my saviour....' she mumbled pathetically. At intervals, she
screamed, 'Papa, look the monster is at large, he is coming to
seize me with his fierce claws, batter me and devour me.
Swami, save your daughter or let me die before my death.'
Having watched and nursed her during the schizophrenic
attacks I simply dreaded to think about the present state of her
mind. Was it all a symptom of a relapse of her disease? I
wondered. And such a thing happening at a place thousands of
miles away from home and while I was on a journey, plunged
me into a condition of utter nervousness, anxiety and
helplessness. What was most disturbing was that Baba, who
had healed her a year earlier was presently at Whitefield and
it was left to me to manage the difficult situation arising out of
the possible relapse of the dreaded disease.

I remembered the scene in the interview room a year ago
when Swami had lovingly consoled me and had given his
divine assurances that he would set everything right and that
Rashmee would improve and be gradually cured.
Furthermore, he had advised my wife to think of giving her
away in marriage to a suitable groom. Was all this mere
moonshine? I wondered. Was his grace a temporary
phenomenon, something wrought by sheer chance or
coincidence? Anyway, I brushed aside such thoughts for the
moment and prayed to Baba to spare me the ordeal of facing
the first-rate crisis that stared me full in the face.

It was a night of the full moon. Rashmee had drifted to the
bosom of restful sleep and a faint moonbeam, coming through
the window, fell on her face. How utterly naive and defenceless
she looked. What wrongs had she done in her past lives that
she had been the victim of a fell disease like schizophrenia?
People said that the words of Swami seldom were proved to be
untrue. What he said came to pass inevitably. Why, then, this
reversion? Was there something lacking in us that we were
being forced to go from ordeal to ordeal? Was our testing time
not over yet?

I opened the door and walked to the terrace. The moonlight
had woven patterns on the *ashram* ground and illumined the
domes of temples and buildings. A soft westerly breeze blew
from across the lofty hills and the nearby Chitravati river. My

wife, who was awake, came to join me. I wanted to share my thoughts with her. I cast a glance at her serene face and fairly composed expression of her eyes. I said in a feeble voice, 'What shall we do now? You remember how ten years back, when she had suffered the first attack, similar symptoms were witnessed initially? She talked incoherently and felt haunted and scared and ran out on the streets in sheer panic. She had such fantastic hallucinations, a series of them and had to be hospitalised as a last resort after her serious relapse at Shimla. But here I find it too much for me to withstand it all. I have neither the resources nor the strength to enable me to fight it out. What shall I do?' I cried in a desperate tone. Unruffled and composed within herself my wife said, 'Who are you to think of doing anything? Don't you have faith in Baba and his divinity? Leave everything to him and he will do the rest. He is father, mother and everything for Rashmee. He will see to it that she does not get the attack or if she gets it, it is not ours, but Swami's business to cure her and restore the sanity of her mind. I am not the least worried, rather I long to have a glimpse of that radiant sun whose beams have transformed my life,' my wife whispered quietly.

But, the oncoming disease left its mark on the victim, poor Rashmee! Early at dawn before sunrise, in the uncertain hour of twilight we packed our belongings and took the first bus bound for Dharmavaram, reaching there just in time to catch the Hyderabad-Bangalore express. In the crowded second class compartment, we somehow found a space in the corner and spread a sheet on the wooden seat and asked Rashmee to lie down on it. As she had had a disturbed sleep in the night, she soon lapsed into sleep. I fondly hoped that she would get a fair measure of equipoise and tranquillity after some sleep. But my hope was belied. The clamour of the wayside stations and the huge rush of passengers boarding the train disturbed her sleep. Some very foolish and quarrelsome ladies even shook her body violently and forced her to rise and make room for them. Rashmee looked at the scene with apparent displeasure and seemed to be bewildered. 'Mother, how far is Bangalore? I am feeling rather hungry and famished. We have already missed our lunch, haven't we?' she asked, turning towards me.

'I suppose there are only a couple of stations to pass by before we reach the terminus. Food was available at Hindupur, but you were asleep and I did not think it proper to wake you up. We will have a shower at the waiting room and will have a high tea,' I said.

'Papa, shall you take me to Whitefield in the evening to enable me to have the *darshan* of Swami? I have been having sinister dreams in my fitful sleep and my body and soul seem to be torn asunder. I tell you, we must stay in a posh hotel at Bangalore, not in lousy hotels with limited space, inadequate ventilators and ramshackle furniture. The demon I spoke of earlier is still after my blood. He is pursuing me all along,' Rashmee said in a frightened tone. I tried my best to assuage her fear. 'Why should you fear when you are so close to Swami? Perhaps, the long journey and loss of sleep and the feverish movements have generated doubts in your mind. But be assured that no demon or monster can ever come near you when Baba is your protector. You will see him sooner than you imagine. You know, God is as restless and keen on meeting His *bhakta,* just as the *bhakta,* on his part, runs towards Him fired by purest love and strongest devotion.'

'Do you think Baba shall grant me the boons I intend asking him for?'

'Of course, I have no doubt about it,' I whispered. I saw the mental emptiness deepening in her eyes and signs of tension writ large over her face.

At the Bangalore junction, we alighted from the train and moved to the second class waiting room to wash ourselves. I ordered tea and snacks in order to get refreshed after the tiring and anxious journey. It was already afternoon, the sun slanting towards the west. The din of the station and shrill noise of trains moving in and out with loud and resonant whistles surrounded us. Rashmee looked fairly tense and agitated, heaven alone knew for what reason. And to me, it seemed as though it was a lull before the storm. After finishing the tea and snacks which consisted of cakes and ice-cream, we came out of the station and hired a scooter to go to Kapila Hotel round the corner of the main bazar. It was the same hotel where we had put up last year, a neat and decent place with large spacious rooms and a terrace of a fair size. The manager

of the hotel, a tall, handsome person, recognised me and
greeted us warmly.

'Are you going to Prasanthi Nilayam, sir? But Baba is
presently at Whitefield,' he said genially.

'No, I am coming from Puttaparthi. And our destination is
Brindavan,' I said and we entered the room which was shown
to us. It was dark now and I switched on the light. A quick
glance was enough to show that the room was not as good as I
had expected it to be. The two beds lay very close to each other
and the distemper on the walls and ceiling had faded. The
furniture was sparse and the upholstery on the sofa looked
dirty and antique. The terrace, opening out on the balcony,
was narrow and congested. The clamour of the city was
incessant and disturbed the privacy of the room. Not satisfied
by the quality of the room I asked the manager if he could offer
us a better room than this one.

'I am frightfully sorry, sir. This is the peak season so far as
we are concerned. The heat in the plains and everywhere in
the towns and cities of the south is mounting and people come
to Bangalore which is a hill station in its own right. All the
rooms are occupied. Only this one remained vacant and you
are fortunate to get this one. I tell you, sir, do please put up
with it for tonight. A good room is likely to be vacated
tomorrow morning. We will shift you there. I hope you won't
mind the inconvenience,' the manager said politely and
withdrew.

'I suppose we have no option in the matter. Let us spend
the night here. Tomorrow we shall shift elsewhere,' I said.

Rashmee, who was listening to my conversation with the
manager, became rather restive and exasperated.

She suddenly lost her balance and shouted. 'No, no, never.
I shan't stay a minute in this nasty hotel. It is no better than a
prison house. The monster is still pursuing me. I must run
away... see... see... like this. Baba, I am coming... wait, wait...'

Before I could comprehend what she meant, she flung open
the exit and rushed down the stairs. My wife simply watched
on and closed her eyes. I ran towards the exit and the
staircase. 'I am going to bring her back... you just stay here. I
shall be back soon,' I told my wife. The next moment I was
standing on the pavement. A crowd flowed by and the

cavalcade of cars, taxis, two-wheelers, trucks and *tongas*
passed on the broad street. Rashmee saw me coming towards
her and screamed, 'Leave me alone! Mind you own business!'
she shouted from the edge of the sidewalk, ready to step on to
the street. The signal lights turned red and green alternately,
but Rashmee, in her present state of frenzy was oblivious of it
all.

I made the last effort to restrain her. 'Rashmee, wait a
minute. You want to change the hotel and go to Whitefield.
Please wait. I will take you there.'

'No, you can't befool or deceive me anymore. Enough is
enough. You are not my father. I disown you. Baba is my
father, my saviour. So get back and let me run to Baba,' she
screamed. The passing traffic rolled by and the business of the
world went on in its usual, metallic rhythm. Bangalore,
though not a metropolis like Bombay, Calcutta or Delhi, is a
fairly large and busy city, the nerve centre of business and
industry. I noticed that Rashmee ran like a frightened deer on
the sidewalk and took a turn towards a semi-dark, less
crowded street. I ran after her and overtaking her, caught hold
of her hand. I admonished her. 'What are you up to, crazy girl?
What will Baba think of you if you behave thus?' I blurted out.

But she was as frantic as before and extricating her hand
from my grasp forcefully, she ran on the street towards the
darker region. I ran breathlessly after her, hoping desperately
to save her from accident or disaster. But I was myself feeling
faint and nervous and my energy was nearly sapped. She was
running far away from me now and there was the rumble of
darkness on darkness beyond. A *tonga*, coming from the
opposite direction stopped on the street and the *tonga* driver
accosted Rashmee: 'What's the matter, sister? Why are you
running on the street at this time of the night?'

Rashmee stopped running and looked at the *tonga* and its
driver with a sense of relief. 'Save me from the monster who is
following me,' she said in a voice trembling.

'Who is he?' asked the driver.

'You don't know him... the flaming monster,' she said. By
that time I reached the spot.

'What is it sir?' asked the driver. 'The girl seems to be in
great fright.'

'Yes, brother. She's my daughter. She is mentally unsound. I am a stranger here. I am at a loss to understand how to manage the situation,' I said.

'Let me try. I will help you if I can,' he said. Then, turning towards Rashmee, he said tenderly, 'Sister, do please mount the *tonga*. I will take you wherever you want to go.'

Rashmee climbed into the back seat of the *tonga* and the driver asked me to come and sit on the front seat by his side.

'No, no, don't allow him. He will deliver me to the monster. I want to go to Sai Baba,' she said firmly.

The *tonga* driver tried to persuade her, but she did not allow me to sit on the *tonga*. The driver said to me, 'See, I will drive the *tonga* at a slow speed. You can follow us. I will take her to a hospital which is near the Bangalore junction.' The driver directed the horse to move on at a slow trot. I had hard time following the *tonga*. All kinds of dismal thoughts came into my mind. What if the driver runs away with her? After all, he is a complete stranger to me. How can I trust him? However, since there was no option left to me, I ran on the street, keeping in sight the moving *tonga* which stopped near a large building which was the hospital. With the help of the *tonga* driver, I took Rashmee to the emergency counter. The nurse on duty said apologetically that it was not a hospital for the treatment of mental diseases. She strongly advised me to take her to the famous Institute of Mental Diseases (NIMHANS) situated in the outskirts of Bangalore.

Rashmee was trying hard to run away once again, but the *tonga* driver was able to control her and prevent her from running. She seemed to respond positively to his directions, but flew into a rage whenever I intervened to say something. The *tonga* driver proved to be a messiah in disguise. He offered to accompany us to the Institute of Mental Health. He left his *tonga* in the hospital premises and hired a taxi for me. He sat by the side of Rashmee on the back seat and coaxed her to submission. We reached the Institute which was twenty kilometres away. There at the gate of the Institute, the driver took leave of us. When I offered him some money, he politely refused, saying, 'You are in distress, sir. Is she not my sister? It is my solemn duty to help you. God will be pleased by my overt or barely noticed kindness. So long.' He waved his hand and disappeared in the darkness of the night. I looked at my wrist watch. It was nine p.m. I took Rashmee to the doctor on duty. He asked me to take the patient to the waiting lounge for the night and bring her back for examination at eight a.m. next morning when the senior consultant would be available. As I walked towards the waiting lounge, the doctor said, 'Do keep a close watch on the patient all night. It is common for the mentally afflicted patients to break all shackles and run out to the streets.'

The lounge was a large hall with a number of benches on both sides, very much like a railway waiting room. Lots of women were sleeping on the floor. Their male attendants either sat or squatted on the adjoining verandah. I asked Rashmee to lie down on a vacant bench. I sat at a place on the verandah from where I could observe her.

What a strange and tragic predicament I was in! It seemed to me as though I was standing on the bank of the river Styx besides Hades. It was the twilight region of the underworld, the *inferno* peopled by anxious, worried women who had lost the sanity of their minds for a variety of reasons, lack of love, the traumas of early childhood, adolescence or youth or some unmitigated shock and tragedy in their lives. And I was destined to bring my daughter here in the dark time of the night while my wife must be waiting in the unfamiliar environment of a hotel for our early return. I also thought of the strange irony of the situation. Sri Sathya Sai Baba, whom we had come to see, was living not very far and could be reached physically in less than three to four hours. But at present the distance seemed to be insurmountable, a gulf that could not be bridged. Surely, my wife must be wondering what had kept us at bay. And the ordeal was before me. I felt faint and weary and stretched myself on the floor. I lapsed into an instant sleep in spite of my best efforts to keep awake. When I woke up after half an hour or so, I got the shock of my life. I looked at the bench on which Rashmee was sleeping. The bench was empty. I looked around closely but there was no trace of the girl.

I paced up and down the verandah and gazed into the lawns nearby. Panic gripped my mind as I marched towards the counter where the doctor on duty was still sitting.

'My daughter, who was sleeping on a bench in the waiting lounge for women, is not there. Have you seen her coming this way?'

'No, look out on the street. Don't say you were not warned. You should have kept a vigil all night. Now make your best efforts to find her. There is a police station close by. You can report to the police. Pray to God and hope for the best,' the doctor said gravely.

I came out on the broad street and walked aimlessly to the right side for a few furlongs and then on the left side also. There was no trace of Rashmee anywhere. The shrill sound of the hooting of a night bird was audible and the murmur of the leaves of the wayside trees sounded like a loud lament. I searched for Rashmee in sheer panic and desperation and all my efforts to locate her came to naught. As a last resort I went to the police station situated in a small building adjacent to the Institute campus. The officer-in-charge listened attentively to my statement and asked me to furnish the first information report in black and white. He seemed to be a sympathetic and kind sort of person.

He said in a soothing tone, 'I can very well understand your predicament. But all I can say at the moment is that your daughter will be restored to you eventually. It is not the first case of this kind when a person suffering from mental illness has run away from the hospital. It is the natural action of a crazed brain to escape, and this too is the natural consequence that the person returns after futile wanderings when the craze or the fever in the brain subsides. It is only in rare cases that the patient meets with some accident or falls a prey to unholy and criminal actions by loafers and vagabonds who prowl at night time to rob, plunder or rape. Let us hope your daughter does not become an unfortunate victim of such hard-hearted criminals. In any case, for tracking her out I shall be sending wireless messages to all police stations in and around Bangalore. You give the name of the hotel where you are staying. Do not worry too much. I have a hunch that she will be traced in the morning, if she is lucky.'

But I could not get a crumb of comfort in my present desolate state of anxiety and exhaustion. The question uppermost in my mind was: 'Shall I see the beloved face of my

daughter again in this life?' The inspector had rightly hinted
at the possibility of her falling a prey to unsocial and criminal
elements. If that happened, it would be a calamity and the
unkindest cut given to me by providence. My thought turned
to Sathya Sai Baba who had affirmed his divinity in no
uncertain terms and had said again and again: 'Bring all your
sorrows and misfortunes to me in the spirit of surrender. I will
make your burdens light and redeem your suffering and give
you eternal bliss.' But the present was critical and calamitous,
the past a series of pain, worries and heartaches, and the
future was futureless. I regretted my decision to come to the
south, leaving the cosy and comfortable and fully sheltered
environment at home where I had the manpower and
resources to deal with such a crisis.

But here in an alien city, without any friend, I walked
aimlessly, treading the pavement covered with fallen yellow
leaves in a dead patrol, the urban dawn wind unresisting, I
again thought of Sri Sathya Sai Baba who seemed to me to be
the only oasis in the desert of wilderness, the only ray of hope
that could scatter the gloom by the sunshine of his grace. I also
thought that if Baba was omniscient and all-knowing, he must
be guarding Rashmee wherever she was, like a good angel. I
thought of returning to the Kapila Hotel where my wife must
be spending hours of anguish in my absence. What shall I tell
her about Rashmee? I wondered. Shall I tell her that the earth
had swallowed her up or that some dark, demonic force had
effaced her existence? Or shall I tell her she has gone to see Sri
Sathya Sai Baba? I could not make up my mind how to inform
her about the mishap that had separated us from our dear
daughter. I wandered on the street up and down in the hope of
spotting Rashmee somewhere. I also went to the Institute
premises and to the women's lounge. But the more I searched
for her, the more disheartened I was, and it looked almost
certain that the tragedy was finely wrought for me, plunging
me into perennial grief. Reaching Kapila Hotel, I climbed the
staircase and tapped at the door of our room with a heavy
heart.

My wife opened the door and asked gently, 'What
happened in the night? Where is Rashmee? Where have you
left her?'

I was too dumb to break the sad news or tell her anything. Tears welled up in my eyes and I slumped on the bed in a heap and burst out into spasmodic sobs.

'Tell me. Don't cry like this. You will break my heart. Tell me. I am prepared to hear the worst news. Has she been run over by a car or a bus? Is she admitted into a hospital? I kept awake the whole night long and the night seemed to be interminable. And now I hear you crying. Tell me what has happened,' she asked stroking my back.

I composed myself somehow and told her of the turn of events leading to the loss of Rashmee.

She listened attentively and her face relaxed from grief to relief.

'Is that all? I imagined something more serious. If she has been lost in the city streets, then it is no great matter. Her guiding angel, Swami, must be with her to show her the way. Do not make yourself ill by crying like a small child. Have faith in Baba. Let us proceed to Whitefield straightaway to be in time there for the morning *darshan*. Write a note for Swami. You may get a chance to hand over to Swami when he comes near you. Hurry up, please. I am going to take a shower. We must start without delay,' my wife said enthusiastically.

I was instantly pacified and marvelled at the attitude of my wife which was so optimistic and positive. Her complete and unquestioning surrender to the divine will had made her capable of smiling even in the face of the greatest crisis and calamity.

We walked to the bus stand near the railway station and boarded the bus going to Whitefield. In the Whitefield campus, the devotees had lined up in a semi-circle in front of a flowering tree with dense green leaves. The ladies occupied one section of the field and the men sat in the other. All eyes were set towards the gate of the building where Baba lived. There was a hush as the familiar figure of Baba appeared in his orange robe and the crown of crescent hair adorning his face. He came near the tree in a graceful and rhythmic movement and then moved along the line. When he came close to me, he looked intently at me for a moment and paused as though to say something. I forwarded the letter towards him and he took it. Then he reassured me with a wave of his hand

and moved ahead. I sat through the *bhajan* session, trying to compose my disturbed mind. The awareness of the tragic event, resulting in the loss of Rashmee, weighed heavily on my consciousness and grief corroded my very being.

After the *bhajan*, I had the least desire to return to Bangalore and to the desolate hotel room and to pine for my lost daughter. So we stayed on at Whitefield for the whole day. We did not feel like taking any nourishment. I could not think of eating when my daughter must be starving somewhere in the city unattended and uncared for. We attended the evening prayers and waited fervently for any tangible assurance from Baba about Rashmee's whereabout and her restoration to us. But Swami took no notice of our presence. All this added up to our grief. As the assembly dispersed, we moved quietly towards the street and to the bus stand. The rush was quite unusual and it was difficult for us to board any bus, specially in our mood of dejection. So, we walked across the railway track to the Whitefield station. Fortunately, a passenger train arrived from Madras and we hurriedly bought the tickets from the counter and found comfortable seats in a compartment. However, nothing seemed to please me. The ominous shadow of foreboding and despair oppressed me and I could not think of anything else. What disturbed me most was that even Swami had chosen to remain detached and indifferent. I had read somewhere the pronouncement of Swami that it was not he who caused pleasure or grief. He is simply a witness, an eternal witness. People get their share of pleasure and pain, of which they themselves are the authors. His saying meant the reiteration of the theory of *karma* exemplified by Lord Krishna in the *Gita*. Still a doubt lurked in my mind. Was it the *karma* of Rashmee that had flung her headlong into the cauldron of suffering and misfortune. Or was it our *karma*, the *karma* of her parents, that accounted for her undoing? Was there no case for divine benediction? I glanced at the receding facade of the hills and trees from the window of the moving train, and I felt like crying. The reality was that Rashmee was lost to us and locating her in the desert wilderness of the granite city and in this wide, wide world was not an easy job. I looked at the emotionless face of my wife and found her to be lost in reverie.

'What are you thinking?' I queried, trying to engage her in conversation. The silence amidst the din and bustle of the compartment was like the silence of the grave, ominous and menacing in the extreme. Besides, I wanted some kind of affirmation from her, I knew that her faith in Baba was deep and abiding and nothing could eclipse it even if the worst came to pass. Perhaps, even the loss of a daughter could not diminish her love and devotion for the Divine. That was perhaps the ideal to be aspired for and attained by a true devotee. But my fractured and tormented self had no such easy faith or spiritual resource to discipline and master my dismal thoughts and wayward feelings. Human love was too much with me and I pined for it endlessly.

My wife looked at me sideways and mumbled. 'Nothing. What is there to think when Swami is there to do all the thinking for us? Since he resides in our hearts, he knows the slightest tremors of our thought and feeling. He knows that we are in grief, and he must be devising ways and means to bring relief. Didn't you notice the sweet and enigmatic smile on his lips as he came near me in the *darshan* line? Our plaint has reached him and our prayers have gone to him already. All we have to do is to wait.'

'Yes, there is nothing else we can do, can we? Human power is so limited but human longing is infinite and unlimited,' I said philosophically.

The train reached Bangalore terminus. We walked out to the busy street in the deepening dusk. The street lamps burnt brightly along the main road. Kapila Hotel was around the corner. But when we came near it, I felt reluctant to go to the hotel room and brood over the tragedy that had separated me from my dear daughter. I preferred to saunter on the crowded thoroughfare and jostle with the flowing sea of humanity. Although I was lonely anywhere, the loneliness on the busy road was not as ominous or menacing as the loneliness of the heart and mind in the privacy of a hotel room. Here at least, there was a sense of flux and movement, although there was tumid apathy and no concentration, only strange, time-ridden faces grimacing at me. I fancied that each face revealed a peculiar preoccupation, reflecting the embrace of grief and joy, obsession with trifles and serious things which the business of living entailed. I remembered the lines of a famous Hindi poet:

This is a passing cavalcade of day and night,
Evenings and mornings, a place for meetings and
separations.
The embrace of joys and sorrows
Which perform their ritual dance in this courtyard.

As I came near the crossroad, the green traffic signal was
on and a thick column of men and women swayed like the
waves of the ocean where the traffic was at a standstill. As I
looked at the swarming crowd I saw a fair, tall figure
resembling Rashmee. Could it be Rashmee really? I wondered
and kept my finger crossed. As the moving figure crossed the
road and emerged on the extremity of the sidewalk on the
other side where my wife and I stood watching her intently, I
recognised her. It was none else but she. A thrill and ecstasy
swept over me in a wave. Words cannot express the joy and
satisfaction I experienced at the moment. It seemed as though
the ocean had yielded up in a whirlpool, my pearl that had
been lost at dawn. My condition was like that of the mariner
who had lost his most precious treasure in the wilderness of
the ocean and been caught into the whirlpool of the stormy
seas with no green isle in sight, but is released by the
devouring waves and spots the lighthouse all of a sudden and
is overjoyed.

Rashmee saw us and stopped. I hugged her close to myself
and whispered, 'Where were you, Rashmee?'

Her mother touched her cheeks and patted her back
affectionately. Rashmee cried and spoke in monosyllables,
'Where were you, Papa? I have been looking for you for hours
since the morning,' she coughed.

'Have you got a cough?' asked her mother.

'Yes, mummy. I had exposure in the small hours of the
morning in the dawn wind.'

'Tell me what happened at the Institute and after?' I
asked, eager to know what had happened actually and how she
had come here so far away from the Institute.

'I will tell you all, Papa. I am myself surprised. When you
asked me to sleep on that bench in the dismal hall, I had a very
brief nap. I woke up with a start and surveyed the immediate
scene. Horrible and ugly faces peered at me and lots of mad
women slept on the adjacent benches and on the ground. Some

old hag cried and screamed in terror. Frightened and terrified, I looked around for you. But you were not to be seen anywhere.'

'Why, I was not far from the lounge. I was sitting near the door and leaned on the wall, tired and exhausted. I may have lapsed into a temporary sleep,' I said.

'But I did not notice. I walked to the gate and out on the deserted street. That monster was still after me in a mad chase, taking giant strides. His shadow loomed after me in the film of darkness. I ran in sheer fright on the pitched road,' Rashmee said in the midst of spasmodic sobs.

'Wait a minute. Shall we remain standing on the busy road? Let's go across to the cafe over there and have some coffee. You may like to eat something. You have not taken any food for the whole day.'

'Who tells you that? Baba gave me something to eat,' she said, smiling mysteriously.

'Baba? What do you mean, Rashmee?' asked her mother.

'Let us first get into that cafe. I will tell you all,' said Rashmee with a lingering smile.

We moved to the cafe which was a neat and decent place. We entered a cabin and ordered coffee.

'Anything to eat, sir?' asked the waiter.

'Bring some sandwiches and cashewnuts,' I said.

I looked at Rashmee and asked her to go on with her narration. She said, 'As I walked past the bus stand, I noticed a bench on the wayside, meant for passengers. I sat there, waiting for a bus, but dozed off in the quiet time of the night. There was no moon in the sky, though some stars shone dimly in the bluish sky. A soft and gentle breeze fanned my cheeks and I closed my eyes to sleep for a while and to escape the onslaught of the hunter, the dragon who had been following me ever since I had landed in Bangalore. When I opened my eyes again, the darkness had dispersed partially and there were white patches of light in the sky and the landscape was bathed in a transluscent glow. I heard a voice, calling me.

' "Why are you sitting here, daughter? So early in the morning and alone?"

'I raised my eyes to see who was speaking to me. I saw a *sadhu,* a fakir wearing a long *kurta* and a scarf-like *kafni* tied around his head. His features were brown and baked, but his eyes were brimming with affection. At that time I did not recognise him. But now I can make a fair guess... he was none other than Baba. I had seen the photograph of Shirdi Sai Baba in our shrine at Muzaffarpur. It seemed that he had stepped out of the picture frame to help me in the hour of my need. I felt attracted towards him instinctively as his manner of speaking was so tender, gentle and affectionate.

' "Baba, I have lost my way," I said.

' "Where do you want to go?" asked the fakir.

' "My parents are putting up in a hotel near the Bangalore station. My father was with me, but he seems to have left me," I said.

' "Never mind. I will show you the way to Bangalore. It is pretty far from here and you can't make it on foot. The first bus will come from that direction and take you to the railway station. Do you have money to pay the bus fare?"

' "No, Baba. I have none," I muttered.

' "Don't worry. Take this," he said tenderly, and stretched his hand. It was a two-rupee note. I took it. The fakir further said, "Do you like to eat groundnuts? I have some. Take a handful. You need it. I know you are hungry," he said and retreated to the shady pavement under the eucalyptus tree and disappeared. Soon the light improved and a number of passengers came up to the bus stand. The city bus bound for Bangalore came when the siren of a nearby factory hooted, announcing the break of the day. I boarded the bus and reached the railway station in half an hour. I had not noted the name of the hotel where we were staying. So, I have been walking on the street ever since the morning. I spent some time watching the posters in the cinema hall and surveying the bazar scene. Perhaps I had exposure to the cold at the bus stand,' she said, coughing.

'Wait a minute, dear. I am going to get some cough syrup for you. Let us go to the hotel and have some rest. We will go to Whitefield.'

'No, no, no, never to that hotel again. Let us go to see Baba right now,' Rashmee shouted and rose from her seat. She ran out of the cabin. I rushed towards her to restrain her. But she was in such a frenzy that it was difficult to manage her. The customers in the cafe and the manager watched us with amusement.

'She seems to be out of her mind,' comented the manager. He said, 'Sir, there is no point in struggling with her. You better take her to the Institute for Mental Diseases which is an excellent place. She will be all right with treatment. You seem to be strangers here. Are you from the north? Take my advice, otherwise you will come to grief.'

By that time, my wife had joined me. After a hurried consultation with her, I decided to take Rashmee to the mental hospital as it appeared to be extremely difficult to control her. Her mental condition caused great anxiety. However, my wife was averse to the idea of getting her admitted to the hospital. She wanted that we should take her to Whitefield and leave everything to Baba. But the present moment was critical. Rashmee seemed to be under a fresh spell of schizophrenic mania and the danger of her being a victim of some accident seemed imminent. So I resolved to take her to the Institute once again. I called a taxi and forcibly put Rashmee into it. 'Come on in, dear, we are going to Whitefield,' I said, trying to soothe her.

But she looked restive and depressed and burst into screams when the taxi stopped near the gate of the Institute.

Fortunately, the senior consultant was available. He had the detailed case history and examined Rashmee thoroughly. He asked the matron to take Rashmee to the ward and give her some injection. He called me to his chamber and said in a grave and solemn voice, 'I think it is a fit case for hospitalisation. She seems to be in an acute phase of manic depression. That is why the motor activity of the mind has increased. But she will improve with treatment, I am sure.'

'How long would you need to keep in the hospital?' I asked.

'It depends on the pace of improvement. Her's is a chronic case and may take three months' time for good improvement,' the psychiatrist said.

'Will you treat her by electric shock therapy?' I queried.

'Not necessarily. First we will keep her on tranquillizers and try psychotherapy to find out the cause of her derangement. Shall we admit her?' said the consultant.

'My problem is that I am not a resident in this part of the country. I am a Professor of English serving in Bihar. We had come here on a trip to see Sri Sathya Sai Baba. In the meantime, she had the attack and I am having a hard time. All I want is that she should improve sufficiently in a week so that I can take her back home. As for long hospitalisation, there are facilities at Ranchi. I hope you understand what I mean,' I said.

'All right. We shall try our level best,' the consultant said and directed me to go to the office and pay the charges for a week. This done, we went to the ward where I found the matron. Recognising me, she said, 'Your daughter is sleeping now. She will be much better when she wakes up. The treatment will do her a world of good.'

'She will be here just for a week. We have to go back home to Bihar. I hope she registers enough improvement so that we can manage the longish journey without trouble,' I said.

'Do not worry. God willing, she will be reasonably well in a week's time. In a disease like schizophrenia, there is no lasting or permanent cure anyway. All we can do is to keep the patient calm and serene within manageable limits.'

'Okay. We will come again in the evening,' I said.

'Please do. You will find her receptive and much more tranquil. Come at four o'clock which is the time for meeting the patients,' the matron said.

'May I have a look at her?' I queried.

'You may, but as I said, she is fast asleep under the effect of morphia. I know how you feel. All parents feel that way when they have to part with their offspring even temporarily. But this is a sanatorium for the healing of diseased and frenzied minds. Go in peace and come each day in the evenings to see the progress in the mental condition of your daughter. Believe me, she will be well. All manner of things shall be well,' said the matron.

We came out of the Institute and moved towards the bus stand. As Rashmee had said, there was a bench for the passengers to sit on. A few yards to the right was a tall eucalyptus tree. Did Baba actually come to this place to render help and assistance to Rashmee as she had described? Or was it just a conceit of her feverish mind and a play of phantasy? I wondered. Anyway from what I had read about Baba in the numerous books relating the experiences of devotees, there seemed to be no reason to doubt the authenticity of Rashmee's statement.

We went to the hotel and after taking a shower prepared ourselves to go to Whitefield. This time we took a train which reached Whitefield. We walked up to the Brindavan and occupied a place in the *darshan* line. Swami emerged at the gate of his bungalow and walked along the row of devotees. He stopped near me and looked at me intently. His eyes kindled and he spoke in a sibilant whisper, 'How nice to meet her! Are you happy now?' He waited for a moment in front of me so as to give me an opportunity to touch his lotus feet. A tear fell from my eyes on those sacred feet. He looked at me compassionately. I remembered his pronouncement: 'If you shed one tear, I will shed a hundred tears!' When the *bhajan* session commenced, I was buoyant in spirit. I felt convinced God never lets down His devotees. He is always with us and is ever ready to help us like a father and mother.

After the *bhajan* I spoke to my wife about what Baba had told me. She was very happy. 'Glory be to God. He gives us trouble so as to test us which often is an ordeal by fire. He has himself said that mankind invites pain to itself and bears the cross all the time. But he is always there—up, above, below, in front and behind—and protects us from all dangers and disasters. What one needs is to leave the navigation of the boat of one's life to his deft hands. Rashmee may be crazed, indulging in daydreams, fancies and conceits, but one thing is certain; Baba must have appeared to aid her to point out the way. She is more devoted to Baba than we imagine.'

'Oh, yes, I have no doubt about that. The girl is exceptionally gentle and pure-hearted. I often wonder why God has ordained so much of suffering to her that fits her like a crown. Can a cross be a coronet?' I said, musing over the lot of Rashmee. In other words, her coronet has been her cross. My heart bleeds for her. I tell you honestly when I saw her coming with the melee of the bunch of men and women, it seemed to me that the sea had yielded up the precious pearl I had lost at the hands of a cruel and recalcitrant destiny. I beheld her coming with a sense of wonder on the pavement. Her coming

restored and marked the gradual return of life to a mind
benumbed by sorrow and grief, I felt the upsurge of the images
of tenderness in her hestitant, delicate movements. It was
indeed my awakening from a trance, as it were. Automatically,
the images from T.S. Eliot's beautiful poem "Marina—The
dramatic monologue of old King Pericles" and meditates on
recovery of his daughter—miraculously returned from the
dead:

> What sea what shore what grey rocks and what islands
> What water lapping the bow
> And scent of pine and the woodthrush singing through the
> fog.
> What images return
> O my daughter....

T.S. Eliot, Marina

I paused and my voice faltered. I added, 'How tragic that I
had to put her there in that dark chamber of mentally
deranged and incapacitated women!' I sighed sadly.

'Remember, it is only for her benefit. Perhaps Baba has
arranged it so with a design. You will see, something good is
bound to come out of it,' my wife said with her usual sense of
optimism.

'I don't know. I know just this that the season of our grief
continues unabated.'

'Baba will see to it that the shadow of grief is lifted and the
sunshine of his grace brings wishes for relief. Have you not
heard the saying "There may be delay in the court of God, but
there cannot be injustice"? Besides, nature also confirms the
fact that after rain there is sunshine,' my wife spoke
animatedly. We proceeded to Bangalore with a lighter heart
and hoped for the best. We changed buses at the station and
reached the premises of the Institute for Mental Health. We
straightaway went to the female ward. Rashmee was talking
with a girl of her own age. She saw us and came towards us.
We walked to the spacious lawn in front of the ward.

A casual look at her was enough to gather the impression
that she was fairly calm and unruffled. I asked her if she had
slept well and had a decent meal. She nodded her head quietly.
However, she complained about the quality of the food. She

referred to Kamala, the girl, with whom she was talking earlier. 'She gets special food on payment from the canteen since the special food is prepared for the doctors and patients who belong to rich and high class families. You know, Papa, Kamala is an artist. She does Bharata Natyam very well. She had offered to teach me. Her mind has been disturbed on account of an unsuccessful love affair. Her boyfriend did not keep his word to wed her and she attempted to end her life by swallowing an overdose of sleeping pills. She was saved by her doctor, but her mental condition and sanity have been affected. Why does life treat sensitive and good souls thus to bring ruin to noble lives?'

'All this happens as God wills it so,' her mother said.

'No, no, I can't believe in such excuses. Look, Papa and you have always tried to get rid of me. First you sent me to the Ranchi hospital and now you have placed me here among these cursed imbeciles. You did not even care to take me to Whitefield as you had promised to do. Instead you have put me here in an asylum. You have treated me very shabbily, indeed.

'This is not true, dear Rashmee. You know how much your Papa loves you. Whatever he does is for your welfare. But sometimes one is dismayed by a series of sad and tragic events and one is forced to take harsh and unpleasant decisions. You do not know how disconsolate we feel without you and you cannot imagine the quantum of our grief. All we want is your happiness and well-being. Since you have pleased Baba, the Lord of the universe, by your *bhakti* and purity of heart, he has always been at your beck and call, your saviour. So, shun gloomy thoughts and look forward to the future with hope and faith,' her mother spoke to her fervently.

Her words seemed to have the desired effect on Rashmee. Her features relaxed from grief to relief. She said, 'If I am a true devotee of Baba and his favourite daughter, he will shower the nectar of his grace on me. You can be sure of that.'

'There is no doubt about that,' I assented.

I went to the manager of the canteen and deposited some money for supplying the special menu of food for Rashmee for a week. Having done this, I came back to the lawn where I had left Rashmee and her mother. The time of the interview was soon over. The matron met us on the verandah as we were leaving. She greeted me with a smile and informed me, 'Your daughter is fast improving. She is responding to treatment fairly well and is quite subdued and normal. The psychoanalysis is going on very well and we expect to get a breakthrough soon. The psychotherapist is fascinated by her case. She seems to be extraordinarily sensitive and possessed of a fine sensibility. She could have distinguished herself in literature, music and the arts but for her crippling disease. She has a deep-seated inferiority complex and hungers for affection all the time. Something must have gone wrong somewhere. Now she is on the verge of enlightenment as a new element has entered her life—religious faith. She says she is a devotee of Sri Sathya Sai Baba. She may be redeemed possibly. We only hope that she does not develop religious frenzy or mania. Her excessive preoccupation with Sai Baba may cut both ways—complete normalcy or yet another reversal or relapse. She is not tired of talking about Baba and declares that she is the daughter of Baba and he gives her *darshan* in dreams. Now tell me if she had any other obsession before.'

'Yes, at one time she was obsessed with the idea of joining the film industry as an actress. She lived under the illusion that she was talented and could shine as an outstanding and great actress,' I said.

'I will tell the psychotherapist. This confirms the hunch that her mental ailment has much to do with frustration, the wide gulf between what might have been and what has been. The cleavage that exists between dream and reality has caused the split and the rent in her mind. The psychoanalyst is a genial and affectionate person and has been successful in establishing rapport with her. The next two or three sittings may prove to be crucial. Thank you for giving us this information.' The matron directed Rashmee to go to the lounge of the female ward where Kamala was waiting for her.

We returned to our hotel and slept quite well that night. I discussed future plans with my wife. As the summer vacation was coming to a close, we thought it proper to book our train reservation for early next week. However, it was necessary to go to Whitefield for a *darshan* of Swami. I was quite hopeful that Rashmee would register sufficient improvement in her mental state next week to be able to undertake the long journey without creating problems on the way.

We went to Brindavan the next morning and attended the *bhajan* session. Sri Sathya Sai Baba sat under the banyan tree on a chair and swayed his hands to the rhythm of the devotional song. 'There is no peace or joy without Sai *bhajan*. There is no one in the world whom one can call one's own except Sainath.' The theme of the *bhajan* moved me profoundly and struck a tender chord in my heart. Although this time our trip to Prasanthi Nilayam and Bangalore was neither salutary nor pleasant since it had plunged us into a morass of gloom and despair, its outcome had fortified our faith in the supreme power of God and in His endless love and compassion for His devotees. The *avatar* who had been incarnated in flesh at Puttaparthi had demonstrated that he had all the sixteen *gunas* or attributes of a full *avatar* like Krishna.

By the grace of the Lord the journey back to Muzaffarpur was, by and large, peaceful. Rashmee slept most of the time and was generally cheerful. However, she expressed her anguish and yearning for Baba and regretted the fact that she was deprived of the chance to have the *darshan* of Baba either at Prasanthi Nilayam or at Bangalore.

'But you did see him in person at the bus stand near the hospital,' I said, trying to assuage her feeling of anguish and regret.

'Oh, yes. But he appeared in another guise and I could not recognise him immediately. How I missed my chance. I should have knelt down at his lotus feet and asked for my boon. Now I am returning high and dry. I hate to be at Muzaffarpur. It has been a place of disaffection for me,' Rashmee said wearily.

'Rashmee, all places are the same. Happiness lies within. If you are enchanted with, and live perpetually in, the thought and meditation of the divine, it confers eternity on the moment and bathes you in perennial joy,' I said.

'You are right, Papa. I lead a blissful existence in spite of the desolation that has been threatening my existence occasionally.'

'Forget about it, my dear. Even your desolation will begin to make a better life,' I assured her.

Back at Muzaffarpur, while I picked up the threads of my work and duties in the Department, my wife resumed her work as the convener of the Mahila section of the Sathya Sewa Organisation. A temple for Baba had been constructed near the Women's College in a quiet corner of the town and regular *bhajans* and *Narayan Sewa* were held on Sundays. My wife was the moving spirit behind it and she took Rashmee along with her to assist her in the service. Time passed fairly smoothly and uneventfully. Rashmee displayed a greater sense of involvement and participation in all that was going on around her. She described her experience of meeting Sri Sathya Sai Baba at the bus stand in Bangalore and when she narrated her tale, there was a glow on her face. Her life now seemed to acquire an altogether new dimension and meaning. Having gone through a temporary reversion, she had emerged stronger and was filled with radiant light and the glow of faith and love. The result of this new-found equanimity was that she seldom fretted or fumed, much less raged against the circumstances of her being. She showed a greater sense of acceptance than before and took everything, adverse or favourable, as the glorious expression of the highest and manifestation of divine will. Weeks passed and the indications, coming from Swami, were once again manifest in the form of *vibhuti*, *kumkum* and *amrita* and I attributed the present spell of comparative peace and serenity in the family to the mercy and kindness of Baba. In fact, we could not think of life without him and saw his hidden hand in everything that happened to us.

I took comfort in the thought that temporary reversions were not that undesirable and, therefore, not to be dreaded. In essence, they fortified and cemented our belief in the divine essence. They kindled the flame of our faith and revived the life of the spirit. The turn of events in Bangalore had been a calamitous one and could have resulted in the greatest tragedy of our life; but Swami saw to it that Rashmee was restored to us quite safe and sound. Rashmee, who had been put in the mental hospital had come out in a much more composed frame of mind. So far as my wife was concerned, her unflinching faith and love for Baba forced the Lord not only to pull us out from possible mourning to morning. My own central dilemma and spiritual miasma had been scattered and I felt as though Baba has become integral to my consciousness and I was getting as close to the idea of total surrender to the divine as one could possibly get. I realised that my griefs had finally become divine because it was mainly by their instrumentality that I had cultivated such nearness to God. I remembered the lines of Vaughan's poem:

> Yes, if as thou does melt, and with thy train
> Of drops make soft the earth, my eyes could weep
> O'er my hard heart, that's bound up, and asleep,
> Perhaps at last (Some such showers past)
> My God would give a Sunshine after raine.
>
> Henry Vaughan, *The Shower*, Stanza iii

The miracle, of course, is wrought by love. When divine grace descends, all grief melts away:

> Love only can with quick access
>   Unlock the way,
>   all else stray
> The smoke, and Exhalatations of the breast
>
> Henry Vaughan, *The Shower*

> How fresh, O Lord, how sweet and clean
> Are thy return. Ev'n as the flowers in spring;
> To which, besides their own demean,
> The late-past frosts tributes of pleasure bring.
> Grief melts away
> Like snow in May.
> As if there were no such cold thing.
>
> George Herbert, *The Flower*

Ever since the miracle restoring Rashmee to me, and Baba's sure and certain hand in bringing about the vital and much needed relief, I felt waves and waves surging towards him. All my doubts, distractions, waverings and dilemmas melted like dewdrops in the heat of the luminous sun and I looked towards God with anxious love inflamed. The loving heart needs affirmations and return of love and when this happens life becomes a blazing torch to illuminate the spiritual path towards attitude and blessedness. Once having tested the bliss of divine affirmation, one can wait until eternity.

The communion with God becomes easy and intimate as in the case of the Sufi poet, Rumi:

He said, 'Who is at the door,' said I, 'Thy humble slave.'
He said, 'What business have you?' said I, 'Lord, to greet thee.'
He said, 'How long will you push?' said I: 'Till thou call.'
He said: 'How long will you glow?' said I: 'Till resurrection.'
            Rumi, *Diwani-Shams-Tabriz*, Trans. R.A. Nicholson

Indeed I had found an anchor for the afflicted mind and bruised soul. But the affliction and the bruise were no longer painful. My pain had turned into roses and within my heart burnt for ever the ember of love. Temporary reversions had proved to me to be a blessing in disguise as they kindled the flame of divine love in the inner sanctuary of my heart and put me firmly on the spiritual path. It is indeed the design of God subject to myriad tests. It is only when He finds us resilient and undefeated and steadfast in our love for Him that He shows His infinite grace and love. The purpose of God is to draw us to Himself and the surest way to achieve this is to heap miseries and heart-rending torments which are difficult to bear:

> Full of rebellion I, I would die
> Or fight, or travel, or denie,
> That thou hast aught to do with me.
> O tame my heart;
> To captivate strong holds to thee.
>   George Herbert, *Nature*, i-vi

It is not that the all-powerful and merciful God punishes us merely for His pastime and sport. He gives us the measure of grief in order to chasten and pity us so that we may shine like gold.

When I had lost Rashmee in the wilderness of the city, I had experienced a virtual anaesthesia of feeling and my sense of grief had permeated my consciousness. I had looked for her frantically and had almost given her up as lost, never to be found again. But when I spotted her in the melee of a bunch of men and women, crossing the street, I felt a thrill of ecstasy, the shock of recognition which revealed to me the mysterious ways of providence and the clearest and most concrete of divine help. Later when Rashmee spoke to us about her mysterious meeting with a *fakir*, who was both familiar and yet unidentifiable, I had little difficulty in drawing the inevitable conclusion that it was none other than Sri Sathya Sai Baba who had come to the rescue of Rashmee. This fact was confirmed when Baba himself spoke to me how we had met Rashmee. Furthermore, he had revealed to us his divine powers as a full *avatar* who was always at the beck and call of his devotees *in distress.* It was in this sense that our temporary reversion, although very critical and tormenting in its impact on us, had proved wholesome and rewarding in the ultimate analysis. I remembered the famous passage from T.S. Eliot's *The Dry Salvages:*

> And right action is freedom
> From past and future also.
> For most of us, it is the aim
> Never here to be realised:
> Who are only undefeated
> Because we have gone on trying:
> We, content at the last
> If our temporal reversion nourish
>   (Not too far from the yew tree)
> The life of significant soil.

                    T.S. Eliot, *The Dry Salvages*

6
ALL THIS AND HEAVEN TOO

After that climactic and crucial experience which brought a complete transformation in our lives nothing happened and we lived out our humble lives as unobtrusively as possible. For seven years we lived quietly, succeeded in avoiding notice, living and partly living. We were compelled to wait for a more eventful future and close communion with the Lord. My wife performed her duties for the Sathya Sewa Organisation with a renewed sense of purpose. Rashmee lived a normal existence, free of any mental aberration. And so far as I was concerned, my lifetime's devotion to my noble profession and calling and my scholarly pursuits set a crown upon my achievements and won for me a fair amount of recognition and renown. However, we assigned all these honours and achievements to the grace of our Lord, Sri Sathya Sai Baba. And we worshipped him as God might be, fixed in the certainty of love unchanging. We continued with our frequent visits to Prasanthi Nilayam for the sustenance and renewal of our faith and love and drew energy from the Lord as from the electric charge of battery.

Whenever my faith slackened and the spirit dropped, I recollected and recalled those hours of illumination and the memory of beatitude and felicity brought me back to my elements:

There are hours when there seems to be no past or future,
Only a present moment of pointed light
When you want to burn. When you stretch out your hand
To the flames. They only come once,
Thank God, that kind. Perhaps there is another kind,

I believe, across a whole Tibet of broken stones
That lie, flung up, a lifetime's march.

T.S. Eliot, *The Family Reunion*

Agatha's speech in this play sums up the basic
predicament of all seekers. It was my dream-wish to lie
perennially in the region of that multifoliate flame and burn in
the heat of anxious love inflamed.

In the meantime, a modest proposal came for Rashmee's
marriage from an altogether unexpected quarter. One of my
colleagues in the Department spoke to Rashmee's mother
about his distant cousin. The boy belonged to a good family,
but on account of adverse circumstances, his family had been
brought to the brink of poverty. The father of the boy, who was
a flourishing doctor and owner of a drugstore died
prematurely. The mother and elder brother of the boy
squandered all the funds by reckless spending and even eroded
the capital, leading to the closure and liquidation of the
drugstore. Consequently, the family lost even the wherewithal
to subsist. The boy was not to blame for all this, but had to bear
the brunt of the follies of his elders. His schooling was
discontinued and it seemed that the sins of the mother had
visited the son. My colleague said that he had immense
sympathy for his cousin and suggested that he could persuade
him to marry Rashmee, to the mutual advantage of both.
Although I had my reservations in the matter, my wife
strongly favoured such a match. It all depended on the luck of
the girl and the blessings of Swami. She felt that the boy could
prosper if they were able to set-up a small business for him. So
the issue was clinched in a hurry.

The marriage was a quiet affair without much notice or
fanfare. An agency in a firm was arranged for the boy and
Rashmee went with her husband to live in Allahabad. From
her letters I gathered that she was fairly happy and contented
with her new life although I always nursed a feeling of
scepticism and uncertainty about this hastily contracted
marriage. A daughter was born to Rashmee and she was full of
pride in becoming a mother. She has discovered a new
meaning in life. A son was born to my daughter-in-law and life,
though not very flamboyant or full of rapture, was reasonably
quiet and peaceful.

Time moved on in its own flux and rhythm and I was fast moving towards my sixtieth year when I would have to face the prospect of retirement from service. I had set my heart on settling down at Prasanthi Nilayam to serve at the lotus feet of the Lord. During my visit to it in 1982, I had been requested by Professor Vinayak Krishna Gokak, the founder Vice-Chancellor of Sri Sathya Sai Institute of Higher Learning, to give a talk on Modern British Poetry to a gathering of teachers and intellectuals. The university of which Sri Sathya Sai Baba was Chancellor had come up only recently. The main purpose of this deemed university was to translate into action and give concrete shape to Baba's idea about education. I considered it a singular privilege to be invited to speak to a group of intellectuals. From the warm applause and favourable response from the audience, I could guess that my talk had been well received. As I did not have enough time at my disposal or access to material, I had to base my lecture on my perceptions about contemporary British poetry and my recollection of some relevant passages from the major poets of our time.

In the evening a general meeting was held in the auditorium of Sathya Sai College of Arts and Sciences. The meeting began with the recitation of *bhajans* by the students. The auditorium was full to capacity and the musical chant of *bhajans* imparted an air of serenity and sanctity to the whole environment. Baba arrived soon after and the proceedings of the meeting got under way. Dr. Gokak gave a report about the seminar, relating the main theme of the lectures and giving the names of the speakers and a resume of the talks. When the meeting was over, Baba came out of the auditorium. Everyone stood in reverence. Dr. Gokak followed him, along with some other important functionaries of the university. Professor Gokak paused when he came near me and said, 'Professor Sinha, do please see me in my office before you go back.' I nodded assent. He smiled affectionately and moved on.

When I saw him in the office, he greeted me warmly and said, 'How nice that you accepted my invitation and gave this talk. I have been informed by reliable sources that you did a very good job of it.'

'I tried my best although I was not prepared for it.'

'What are your future plans? When are you expected to retire?'

'A couple of years still to go. I have not yet thought of the future,' I said.

'Do please be in touch with me. I may need your services. I wish to make the Institute a temple of learning in the real sense of the term. We have drawn up the most advanced syllabi, incorporating the frontiers of knowledge in each discipline. The real challenge before me is to recruit devoted and capable teachers. My aim is to fashion the Institute into a top institution in the world. And the circumstances are very propitious indeed. At the helm of affairs is the *avatar* himself whose avowed message and mission is to uplift mankind spiritually. Here the students are a disciplined lot of devotees having studied here right from nursery to high school. It is Swami's love that has conquered all and bound us together in unbreakable bonds of faith and love. An idea has just flashed across my mind. How nice if you could also participate in this adventure in the realm of the spirit and come to serve here as a teacher. We can offer you the coveted chair in English. We cannot hope to get a better person than you. Since you are also a devotee, you will fit in very well in the overall pattern. You think about it dispassionately and let me know so that the formalities can be completed well in advance and you can take up the assignment after you relinquish your post in Bihar University,' Professor Gokak spoke at some length.

'What is there to think about? I shall deem it to be a great honour to be called upon to serve at the lotus feet. In fact, it has been my dream wish. In the course of my long career I have pined to work in ideal conditions. But nowhere have I found the ideal state of affairs. You can take my consent for granted,' I said, beaming with joy.

'Think that it is as good as done. The only snag is that there should be enrolment to the master's course in English, and most important of all, Swami consents to your appointment,' Professor Gokak said with disarming frankness. When I came back to the room in the round building I spoke to my wife about it. She was overjoyed. 'It would be simply wonderful. Who wouldn't rejoice at the prospect of dwelling in heaven?' she said.

A number of visitors came to see me in my room and asked me questions pertaining to my talk on contemporary verse. I also met Dr. N.R. Shashtri who was Reader and Head of the English Department at the college and he seemed to be fairly happy and contented on having joined the Institute, taking long leave from his original post at Osmania University, Hyderabad.

When I returned home I started setting my house in order and finishing all my previous assignments and commitments, preparatory to retirement. I completed the script of two of my novels and signed contracts with my publishers in Delhi and Jaipur. I was very happy indeed with the artistic quality of the two novels and reserved the task of transcreating them into English for the international market, and for worldwide dissemination, to a later date, after retirement. I travelled far and wide in the country on prestigious assignments as a subject expert for the selection of professors and readers in English literature for several universities and the Union Public Service Commission and Ministry of Education. I did all this in humility and was almost reduced to a condition of complete simplicity. It sounded strange and unbelievable to me how imperceptibly I had learnt to shed my overbearing ego even in the face of such commendable achievements. An inner spiritual change had come about me and I functioned as an instrument in the hands of God, to do God's work. And I waited for the wished-for consummation when I would take up the job at Prasanthi Nilayam. Rashmee came to Muzaffarpur with her husband occasionally to see us. When she came to know that I might settle down at Prasanthi Nilayam and do the work of Swami, she became rather sad and nostalgic. 'Papa, will you take me there with you when you go there? I am dying to see Swami. The atmosphere in our home is not very conducive for spiritual discipline and exercise. Shravan is considerate, but he has no love for things spiritual. He is entirely Godless. I am trying my level best to turn him to God, but his *samskars* are those of an atheist.'

'Are you happy, my dear?' I asked.

'I don't know. But anyone who comes between me and Baba cannot claim all my affection. Papa, promise, you will take me to Baba, otherwise there will be an end to me. I cannot

suffer to put up with the long drawn-out consequences of days
and hours and the emotionless years of living amidst the
wreckage of one whom I believed in, to be the most reliable,'
said Rashmee in a sad voice.

'Live in peace, my daughter. I will certainly take you to
Prasanthi Nilayam,' I said, trying to pacify her. However, I felt
disturbed by her adverse references to her husband. I
apprehended that she was not hitting it off well with him but
took it as the initial difficulties in adjustment so common with
newly married couples. I was fascinated to see her little
daughter who was so fair and pretty with large black eyes.
After a week's stay at Muzaffarpur, Rashmee left for
Allahabad.

When she was gone, I spoke to her mother about my doubts
and apprehensions. 'Everything does not seem to be going
smoothly in her conjugal life. She complained to me the other
day,' I sighed.

'You know your daughter, don't you? She always wants to
have her way. She has grown to be obstinate and self-willed.
Her husband is quite considerate, but he is not submissive.
Besides, he has lived so long in poverty and want. So he tends
to suffer from an inferiority complex. Rashmee tries to
dominate over him which he naturally resents. But don't
worry. Living together, they would learn to understand each
other,' my wife said.

'Let us keep our fingers crossed and pray to Baba that the
marriage works,' I said in a sad and weary voice.

'I do not see any point in worrying. We should take life as it
comes. There is nothing else we can do, can we?' she said
calmly.

'No. But we can certainly pray to Baba,' I said.

'Rest assured, that will be done. When we go to live in that
heaven of eternal bliss, we shall leave the luggage of worries
and miseries behind,' my wife said, smiling.

The date of my superannuation drew very close. On that
crucial day, I handed over the charge of the Department to the
seniormost Reader and spoke very warmly and feelingly to my
colleagues and students about the banner of the Department
flying high. I had nurtured it tenderly and given it unique
distinction in all spheres of academic and intellectual

activities. I felt immeasurably sad to part company with
friends, but knowing that life was compounded of such
meetings and partings, I consoled myself.

There was the radiant future before me and I waited to
hear from the Vice-Chancellor of Sri Sathya Sai Institute of
Higher Learning. But no letter came. I received an intimation
from the North Bengal University, Siliguri, West Bengal, that
I had been appointed as a subject expert by the Chancellor on
the Selection Committee for the selection of Professor of
English at that university. I proceeded to Calcutta to attend
the meeting, specially convened there. We interviewed half a
dozen candidates, all belonging to North Bengal University.
They were all Readers, but their performance was not quite up
to the mark. Moreover, none of them possessed a doctorate nor
had they supervised any research leading to the Ph.D. degree,
not to speak of outstanding publications to their credit. So, I
was constrained not to be able to recommend anyone for the
post. Instead the Committee decided to re-advertise the post
and hold another meeting of the Selection Committee next
month.

I came back to Muzaffarpur and checked my mail. There
was a letter from Professor Gokak informing me that
advertisements had been sent to the newspapers, announcing
the commencement of the Master's courses in English
literature. He assured me that even if one student was
admitted to the course, he would offer me the post of Professor
of English and the Chair. Thus, the period of waiting was
prolonged. In the meantime, the scheduled meeting of the
Selection Committee at Calcutta was convened and I was
informed telegraphically to attend it. This time also, the same
set of candidates appeared for the interview and I refrained
from recommending anyone for the coveted position. The other
expert also expressed the same opinion. Thereupon, the Vice-
Chancellor asked me to recommend the name of any other
suitable candidate from among my acquaintances. Before I
could say anything, the other expert said to the Vice-
Chancellor, 'Professor Sinha himself may be available. He has
retired already from his post in Bihar University.' The Vice-
Chancellor said, 'Is that so? Then my problem would be solved.
We can't expect to get any better person than him.' Then,

addressing me, he said, 'What do you say, Professor Sinha? Can you come?'

'What will be the terms and conditions?'

'Five years' contract as here the age of retirement is sixty-five and the salary will be the same that you were getting at the time of retirement at Bihar University. Isn't this fair?'

'I will think about it and let you know in a week,' I said.

So, the dramatic turn of events forced me to land at Siliguri and join the post of Professor of English. I stayed in the university guest house. I had worked there only for ten or fifteen days when the summer vacation commenced and the university was closed. I requested the Vice-Chancellor to allot residential quarters to me so that I could bring my family in July. He readily agreed and expressed his happiness over the fact that I had accepted his invitation and joined the university.

However, Swami did not will it that way. On return from Siliguri to Muzaffarpur, I received an urgent telegram from Professor Gokak intimating me that I was appointed Professor and Head of the English Department at the Institute and that I should join latest by the fifteenth of July, 1985. There was not much to think about now. I sent a letter of resignation to the Vice-Chancellor, North Bengal University, expressing my regrets and proceeded to Prasanthi Nilayam to take over my new assignment. Rashmee joined us later since I had to keep my promise to take her to there for the *darshan* of Baba. Her husband resented this arrangement, but we had our way.

The fifteenth day of July 1985 was the auspicious and fateful day when I joined my post at the Institute and started my obeisance to Swami. It was two paradises in one: being at Prasanthi Nilayam and serving at the lotus feet of the Lord. We were housed in a room at the *ashram* temporarily as the university quarters were in the process of being constructed. I met Dr. Shashtri and other colleagues in the Department and resumed my work. Professor Gokak invited me to discuss the projects and plans for shaping the Department on the ideal pattern which Swami had in mind. He discussed with me the quality and calibre of other members of the Department which consisted of two Readers and two lecturers and one part-time teacher who had had a distinguished career and lived

permanently at the *ashram*. All were devotees of Baba, pure
and serene. It was indeed a pleasure to work with such a
consecrated band of colleagues. In the M.A. course, there was
just one student from Calcutta, West Bengal. He had had his
early schooling at Prasanthi Nilayam and possessed a rich
organic sensibility and critical intelligence of a very high
order. I loved to lecture to him on the diverse fields of
literature. Since the courses were wide-ranging, covering wide
areas and representing the very frontiers in each field, the
teaching work was extremely challenging. I had to work very
hard, but the satisfaction and thrill I got out of teaching
surpassed all other joys. In my whole career, teaching had
never been such a delightful and estatic affair. Indeed, at the
Institute, one worked with one's whole soul alive as work here
was truly prayer. What was the most pleasurable, and much
sought after, thing for most of us was the morning and
afternoon *darshan* of Sri Sathya Sai Baba and attendance at
the evening *bhajans*. As we had no other option, we took our
breakfast and meals at the *ashram* canteen. My granddaughter, Sambhavna, was now five years old. We decided to
get her enrolled in the Sri Sathya Sai Primary School. I met
the Lady Principal in this connection, but she informed me
that admission had closed after the test. Besides, the girl
appeared to be less than five years old. She advised me to
speak to Swami. My wife spoke to Swami one day. Swami came
to her in the *darshan* line and recognising her, said, 'So, are
you happy here?'

'Yes, very much, Swami. What about Sambhavna's
admission?'

'Wait, wait,' said Swami, moving ahead in the line.

Later I spoke to Professor Gokak about it and he directed
the Registrar to intervene in the matter. Mrs. Kaul, the Lady
Principal, had her reservations, but she relented finally on
production of an affidavit about the age. Thus Sambhavna was
placed in the hostel in the school and cried bitterly on being
separated from us. She missed her mother and grandmother,
but eventually in the company of other kids and the
affectionate care of the principal and the other teachers, she
settled down and even enjoyed her time in school.

For my wife, life at the *ashram* meant a complete surrender of the self to the Lord and continual service and self-sacrifice. She sometimes worked in the canteen cutting vegetables or in the campus cleaning the alley walks or assisting the head volunteer in regulating the women's group. She seldom missed the morning *Prabhatpheries* and the *bhajans* during the mornings and evenings. Swami often spoke to her and sometimes even teased her with his playful remarks. In whatever Swami said to her, there was certain evidence of his redemptive love. She had established a nearness with the Lord and never missed an opportunity to touch his lotus feet or give utterance to her problems. All her plaints were Sambhavna or Rashmee.

'Swami, Sambhavna has a hole in her heart, a congenital defect since her birth. The heart specialists at the A.I.I.M.S., New Delhi, have advised open heart surgery. Please, cure her by your grace,' she would say.

'Wait, wait. I have given her *vibhuti*,' Swami said.

'Swami, Rashmee...' she would say.

'Why, isn't she all right now?'

'Yes, Swami by your grace she is fairly normal, but her husband does not do anything. He is not shaping well at all....'

Swami looked grave. 'I had asked you to find a suitable match for her,' Swami said in a solemn tone. 'But you ask things for everyone, but never care to ask anything for yourself.'

'Swami, you have called us to live in this heaven, and all my desires and cravings have ceased. I do not want anything, simply give me the opportunity to serve at the lotus feet,' my wife would say in a sublime and animated tone.

As for Rashmee, she lived at the *ashram* with a sense of ecstasy. She, like her mother, attended the *bhajans* without fail and stood in a corner behind the enclosure, looking at Swami from a distance. As she had some difficulty in sitting on the ground on account of the periodic recurrence of her spine trouble, she generally avoided sitting in that posture. But Swami cast a lingering look at her She received letters from her husband at regular intervals. He wanted her to get back to Allahabad, but Rashmee declined. Since her husband had nearly exhausted all the capital I had given him for the business through reckless spending and was always demanding money from me, I did not take any initiative to send Rashmee to Allahabad for that would have meant further provision of funds to him. I asked Rashmee to inform him that he could himself visit Prasanthi Nilayam and discuss his future plans with us.

As for myself, life was a saga and chronicle of peace and joy. Baba was directly accessible and I could speak to him whenever I wished to, or hand over a letter to him. Often, he stood near me and gave me a chance to touch his lotus feet. Often he was aware of the contents of my note even before I had given it to him. Sambhavna had complained of pain in the chest one evening when he had gone to see her. Perhaps she had strained herself playing on the swing too long. Baba said, 'Don't worry, I have given her *vibhuti.*'

One afternoon, as he came to the verandah of the *mandir*, he asked, 'Where is the Professor of English?' I stood up.

'Where have you come from?' he asked, looking into my eyes.

I was confused and did not know what to say. 'Sit down,' he said, and moved away. I realised later that the question was not as simple as it seemed to be on the surface. I should have said, 'I have come from God, the maker and my goal is God.' I knew from experience that Baba induced the devotee to ponder on the basic questions and find the correct answer.

At Prasanthi Nilayam, the very atmosphere was charged with spirituality and there was something sacred in the air itself. Everyday, there was the spectacle of the continuous influx of devotees from each and every corner of the world. Politicians of every hue and colour, heads of states, central ministers, governors and men of eminence in all fields of life thronged in large numbers; and on special occasions, Swami gave his divine discourses and revealed his knowledge and awareness of all disciplines. He could easily and fluently converse with the foreign devotees in their own language. At the auditorium of the Institute, Baba gave discourses pretty frequently. Often I heard him talk about the intricacies of nuclear physics. On another occasion, he spoke to us about the present state of business administration in America, USSR and Japan from inside knowledge of the subject. When an

official came from the Ministry of Education to expound the
proposal of the Question Bank, Baba surprised him by showing
his awareness of the different aspects of the concept. On one
occasion, on the request of Dr. Jha, a former Vice-Chancellor of
Benares Hindu University, Baba gave us a graphic and
succinct narrative of the life of Tulsidas.

It was amazing to hear him and it seemed as though he
was at the source of all knowledge, because all knowledge
emanated from him. Once he told us that he could speak in
English if he wanted, but he preferred the medium of Telugu
as it was more rhythmic and pliable on his lips. He remarked
that all power lay in his palm. He created a jewel with an
exquisite design and passed it on to the assembled audience.
When it was returned to him he blew over it and it became a
flower. Baba said, pointing to a young student. 'Look, I can
transform this boy into a girl and *vice versa*.' We all held our
breath and gasped. Baba unfurled the national flag at the
university on the independence day and gave an authentic
description of the freedom movement. He presided over the
Annual Sports of the university and enjoyed watching all the
items. He often distributed apples among the teachers,
throwing the apple towards each of us and said, smiling, 'An
apple a day keeps the doctor away.'

Nothing happened at Prasanthi Nilayam without him. He
was indeed the presiding deity of the place, the glory of
Puttaparthi as indeed he was the Lord of the universe and the
cosmos. He was particularly affectionate towards children and
enjoyed their company. He visited the Primary School and
spoke to the kids. Sambhavna was his favourite. Many a time,
he had taken her to the hospital when she was sick and he had
directed the Lady Principal to pay special attention to her and
offer her plenty of fruit and milk. He attended to the minutest
details of life while he was engaged in running the whole
universe. He often spoke of his work in the previous *avatars*
and of the present one, which was the establishment of *Sathya
dharma*, *Shanti* and *Prema* on a firm footing.

The university quarters were ready and allotments were
made by the Vice-Chancellor by drawing lots. The buildings
were three-storeyed mansions in which there were flats of two
bedrooms for each one of us. At Prasanthi Nilayam,

distinctions based on rank or position did not matter. Accommodation for everyone was uniform. I was fortunate to get a flat on the ground floor, but the most auspicious thing about it was that the building was inaugurated by Baba and the *puja* was performed in the flat allotted to me. This was just a matter of coincidence, but it made me feel very good. My wife had the occasion to touch the lotus feet and as someone was taking a series of Baba's photograph, he appeared in one of the photographs in a kneeling posture.

Among some of the notable and important functions I attended at Prasanthi Nilayam, mention must be made of the annual convocation of the Sri Sathya Sai Institute of Higher Learning. Sri S.B. Chavan, the present Home Minister in the Central Government and at that time, Minister of Education in Rajiv Gandhi's Government, was the Chief Guest. Sri Chavan had been a devotee of long standing and visited Puttaparthi very frequently. During the convocation, the pageantry was very impressive. First we assembled at the hall in the *mandir*. Baba was present there and he asked the student volunteer to serve some cold drink to us. Then the procession was formed with Baba at the helm and we proceeded to the specially designed pandal. Baba declared the convocation open and Sri Chavan delivered the address. It was indeed a privilege to me to sit in that august company on the dias and watch every action and gesture of Baba from so close a view.

But the most memorable event indelibly transfixed in my memory was the golden jubilee celebrations of the *avatar's* sixtieth birthday in 1986. It impressed me as truly the most memorable and greatest show on earth. For one thing it attracted, even by the most modest estimate about ten lakhs of people. A whole sea of humanity had surged to the hallowed birthplace of the Lord. It took me nearly an hour to reach the *mandir* from my residence which normally took less than five minutes. Yet by some unseen power, the crowd remained thoroughly disciplined. The crowd converged towards the Hill View Stadium which was the venue of the celebrations. Swami gave his divine discourse in the evenings on moral and spiritual themes and every word he said poured like drops of nectar into the ears of the receptive listeners. Swami had

announced that each and every one who had come to attend
his birthday was his guest and that all should have their
breakfast and meals in the backyard of the *ashram*. The
arrangement for the meals was perfect and the Sewa Dal
volunteers worked round the clock to ensure timely service.
On the morning of November 23 the traditional procession was
taken out with Sai Gita in the vanguard followed by Swami,
the teachers and students and the permanent residents of the
ashram. It was a heavenly sight to watch. In the night *bhajans*
were sung and Swami swayed on the swing. The celebrations
terminated at midnight, marking a landmark and a signpost
in the life of the *avatar*.

Some very important visitors at Prasanthi Nilayam
included Mr. Craxy, the Prime Minister of Italy, King
Birendra of Nepal and Mr. Jayawardhane, the President of Sri
Lanka. It is common knowledge that the former President of
India, Sri R. Venkataraman, used to visit Prasanthi Nilayam
to receive the blessings of Baba. Only recently, he inaugurated
the opening of an airstrip for the landing of small planes and
helicopters at Puttaparthi. The outgoing Prime Minister, Sri
P.V. Narashimha Rao, recently inaugurated the New Sathya
Sai Hospital meant to cater to the needs of the poor. The
hospital is supposed to be one of the best in the world with
foreign specialists in open-heart and kidney surgery, all for the
benefit of the poor who could get treatment free of cost. A great
transformation, amounting to a sea-change has come over the
birthplace of the *avatar*—the small, tiny village of Puttaparthi
in the interior part of Andhra Pradesh. A planetarium has also
come into existence and I had many opportunities to watch the
stars and the comets.

I thought of the linear movement of time and the flux that
was an essential part of the rhythm of creation. Everything
was moving necessarily towards the inevitable close and the
ultimate finale. A time would come probably in the not too
distant future, in the first quarter or the next century when
Puttaparthi would become a place of pilgrimage like Shirdi in
Maharashtra after Shirdi Sai Baba had taken his *samadhi*.
Since the *avatars* transcended the frontiers of time and space,
they were eternally present. Shirdi Sai Baba had declared that
he would speak to his devotees from his tomb and would

continue to guide and protect them. Sri Sathya Sai Baba has
also said that he would live for ninety-five years and after
completing the work for which he has been incarnated upon
the earth, he would leave the scene and that he would appear
in the third incarnation as Prema Sai at Gunaparthi in the
Mandya district of Karnataka. Baba has further said that he
still waited—for all his devotees, who were destined to come to
see him, should come. He has also cautioned that it would be
difficult to come near him as the rush would increase a
thousand-fold. He has given to some of his devotees the picture
of Prema Sai. I thought how fortunate I had been to live there
and see Baba day in and day out.

Words fail me and I cannot adequately relate the quantum
of my bliss and the magnitude of my thankfulness to the Lord
for bestowing such love and grace on me and my family and for
enkindling in me the spark of divine love. I felt as blessed, as
Francis Quarles says:

He gives me wealth; I give him all my vowes;
I give him songs; He gives me length of dayes:
With wreathes of Grace he crowns myconqu' ring browes:
And I, his temples, with a crowne of praise,
Which he accepts as an everlasting signe,
That I my Best-Beloveds am; that He is mine.

Francis Quarles, *Canticles II*, 37-42

I can affirm in a spirit of all humility and self-effacement
that I spent the best and the most glorious years of my life at
Prasanthi Nilayam. I got the highest sense of fruition and
fulfilment through complete immersion in work, earning the
greatest measure of job satisfaction and, what was most
important, the rich feeling of belonging. Truly I was an inmate
of Heaven doing the work of the *avatar* in my humble way. I
had all this and heaven too! As a consequence of some of my
noble and virtuous deeds in the past lives, I was given this
unique honour to be associated with God, who had taken the
human form to redeem mankind and to foster His sincere
devotees. I had come to the place of the round world's imagined
corner from where I could see a vision that was the vision of
beatitude and innocence. Life itself was aglow with the radiant
flame of divine love, ardour and devotion and the past pains,

troubles and turmoils melted away in the fiery glimmer and incandescence of that love. I envisioned a time when the vision of experience would get marked with the primal vision of innocence and beauty. Thus my sojourn at Prasanthi Nilayam made it possible for me to witness the impossible union of the different spheres of existence. That is why I had the privilege of having all this and heaven too which indeed is the fitting conclusion of all human aspirations.

7
THE IMPOSSIBLE UNION OF SPHERES OF EXISTENCE

As everything in this world has a beginning, a middle, and an end, this modest heartwork of mine on a great subject which is no more than a homage to the Lord, who is the Absolute Sole Lord of Life and Death, must also come to a close. But as the poet has said, 'In my beginning is my end.' And he further says:

> We must be still and still moving
> Into another intensity
> For a further union, deeper communion
> Through the dark cold and the empty desolation
> The waves cry, the winds cry, the vast waters
> Of the petrel and the porpoise. In my end is my beginning.
> T.S. Eliot, *Four Quartets*, East Coker, 204-10

In this sense, there is no beginning, or an end. The exploration is constant and eternal:

> We shall not cease from exploration
> And the end of our exploring
> Will be to arrive where we started.
> And know the place for the first time.
> T.S. Eliot, *Four Quartets*, Little Gidding, 239-42

So we must return to the first chapter of this work, muse over the full significance of my climatic and crucial experience of standing face to face with the fell sergeant, Death, and all-merciful Lord, the Saviour. I may make another personal statement in the hope that you will bear with me. In fact, the book has developed into a journal *intimate,* a stringing together of the personal perceptions and feelings of the author in relation to Sri Sathya Sai Baba. What better way can there be to close the narrative on another personal note as a sequel to, and apex and crown of, this subjective saga and chronicle of love and faith?

The Supreme Lord of the universe has incarnated in the human form at Puttaparthi at the present juncture of human history as he had done earlier as Rama and Krishna, but the supreme weapon in his armoury is Love, the force that transfigures and binds all for the, creation of a paradise on earth. A searching look at his sun-like features and radiant face is enough to convince the beholder that in his personality the spheres of existence have found their impossible union. He has the moral righteousness of Rama, the limitless love of Krishna, the compassion of the Christ and the Buddha, and all these have merged together and synthesised into a multifoliate rose. No wonder that one is renewed and transfigured and bathed in the perfume of the rose, meaning love, as one comes in touch with him and burns in the fire of divine love. So, my exhortation to all seekers is, in the words of T.S. Eliot:

> Quick now, here, now, always...
> A condition of complete simplicity
>   (Costing not less than everything)
> And all shall be well and
> All manner of things shall be well
> When the tongues of flame are in-folded
> Into the crowned knot of fire
> And the fire and the rose are one.
>   T.S. Eliot, *Four Quartets*, Little Gidding, 252-60

SAI MESSAGES FOR ONE AND ALL

It is the nature of supreme reality to express itself in concrete, tangible and ever recognisable forms just as it is the nature of the sun, that great planet imperial of the solar system, to send beams of light and heat to each and every corner of the earth. By the same token, when the Creator of the cosmos, the Absolute Lord of the universe incarnates Himself in human form, something momentous and beautiful happens. The purpose of the *avatar* is verily to redeem the sufferings and travails of humanity and to take mankind to the kingdom of heaven. He shows, both by example and precept that man is essentially divine and that his destiny and destination lie in the merger with the Infinite, the Divine Essence for further union and deeper communion.

Thus, Lord Rama lived up to the highest ideals of manhood and has rightly been designated as *Maryada Purusottam*. Lord Krishna enunciated the doctrine of *karma* or disinterested action without caring for the fruits of action, when he admonished Arjuna in the battlefield of Kurukshetra. Even Lord Buddha and Prophet Mohammad, who, according to Sri Sathya Sai Baba, were not *avatars* though they had some divine powers, preached their gospels of utmost beauty and moral clarity in order to put mankind on the road to perfect living. The Fire Sermon and Quran are living embodiments of this extreme moral beauty, blossoming into a religion of love.

Sri Sathya Sai Baba, who, by common consent, is accepted as a full *avatar* with all the sixteen *gunas,* has concentrated on his mission of teaching right from the beginning of his advent.

He has explicitly declared that the first sixteen years of his life will be devoted to *leelas* and the next sixteen years to *mahimas*. And he has stated that the remaining years will be devoted entirely to teaching, whereas the aspect of *leelas* and *mahimas* would continue throughout. One has only to read the eleven volumes of *Sri Sai Speaks*, to taste the veracity of the divine declaration. Reading these volumes is like tasting the sweet nectar and being drenched in the salutary showers of his redemptive love. What is unique and amazing is that his words go straight into our hearts and find resonance there. Truly, these words are the repository of the concentrated wisdom of the *Vedas*, the *Upanishads* and the scriptures, expressed in direct, simple, intimate, effective and homely language, shorn of metaphors and embellishments. Simple comparisons and familiar analogies abound as the only strategy to reinforce the design of the teachings so that the messages sink deep into the central depths of the consciousness of the listener or the reader.

Sri Sathya Sai Baba is a poet in his own right, a great poet who has fashioned and carved out images of unique splendour and beauty in order to drive home his crucial message of *Sathya, dharma, shanthi* and *ahimsa*. And the constellation of his intention is very clear, that is precisely to make man a living flame, a resplendent diamond to shine perennially in the limitless spendour of love. One is reminded of the lines of W.B. Yeats, who said in one of his poems 'Words alone are certain good.' But words are mere husks unless they incarnate and enclose the essence of feeling and experience and are quickened and enlivened by the intensity of lived and felt apprehensions and reflect the sincerity and ardour of a lifetime, burning in every moment. The universal appeal of *Srimad Bhagavad Gita* or the Sermon of the Mount lie expressly in the context in which they were delivered and the full and complete authenticity of the speaker. Since the life of Sri Sathya Sai Baba has all the sanctions of *sathya, dharma, prema, shanthi* and *ahimsa,* his words give us elemental bliss and make us in the likeness of a resplendent diamond, or flame of fire. Given below are some of the gems which may enlighten

the readers and induce them to live by them for the attainment
of wholesome spiritual discipline and bliss.

The *avatar* comes as Man in order to demonstrate that man is
divine, in order to be under the reach of man. The human mind
cannot grasp the Absolute, attributeless principle. It is
abstract and within the reach of speech, mind and intellect.
Love is his instrument, non-violence is his message. He
achieves the correction of the evil-minded through education
and example.

Among the *avatars,* Rama and Krishna are most
meaningful to mankind since man can grasp their examples,
follow their solutions to problems and derive *ananda* through
contemplation of their excellence and teachings.

If I had come only as man like any other man, who would
listen to Me? So I had to come in this human form with more
than human power and wisdom.

The *avatar* is capable of all things at all times, yet he will not
undertake to demonstrate such powers except when
exceptional circumstances demand it and will shower his grace
on a deserving person only.

Like good food that comes to one who has been fasting for the
past ten days, like a heavy downpour of rain that comes to fill
the dried and the empty tanks, like a child coming into a
family which has for long been yearning for children, like a
shower of wealth to a very poor man, Sathya Sai has come to
Puttaparthi when there is total decline of *dharma* among
people.

There are many who observe my actions and start declaring
that my nature is such and such. They are unable to gauge the
sanctity, the majesty and the eternal reality that is Me. The
power of Sai is limitless. It manifests itself for ever. All forms of
power are resident in this Sai palm.

My power is immeasurable. My truth is inexplicable, unfathomable. I am announcing this about Myself, for the need has arisen.

Let Me tell you Mine is no mannerism, miracle or magic. Mine is genuine divine power.

There was no one to know who I am till I created the world, at My pleasure, with one word. Immediately, mountains rose up, rivers started flowing, earth and sky were framed, oceans, sealands and water sheds, sun and moon and deserts sprang up out of Me, out of nowhere to prove My existence. Then came all forms of beings, man, beasts and birds, flying, speaking, hearing. All powers were bestowed upon them under My orders. The first place was granted to mankind and My knowledge was placed in man's mind.

Come, one and all. See Me yourself, for I see Myself in you—all of you are My breath, My life, My soul. You are My forms all. When I love you, I love Myself. When you love yourself, you love Me. I have separated Myself from Myself so that I may love Myself. My beloved ones, you are My own self.

Why fear when I am here? Put all your faith in Me. I shall guide and guard you.

My children, the bird with you, the wings with Me, the foot with you, the way with Me, the eye with you, the form with Me. The thing with you, the dream with Me, the world with you, the heaven with Me. So we are free, so we are bound. So we begin and so we end. You in Me and I in you.

Sathya is what I teach. *Dharma* is the way I love. *Shanthi* is the mark of My personality. *Prema* is My very nature.

I am in you, you are in Me. There is no distance or distinction. You have come to your own home. This is your home. My home is your heart.

Learn to yearn so that you can draw Me to you wherever you are. That is a more rewarding *sadhana* than the journeys. Transform your heart into Prasanthi Nilayam, then I shall certainly come and stay there.

Sri Sathya Sai Baba

I am not Sathya Sai Baba. That is only a name by which you describe Me now. All names are Mine. I am the One God who answers the prayers that rise in human hearts in all languages from all lands, addressed to all forms of deity.

The most significant and important power, let Me tell you, is My *Prema* I may turn the sky into earth and the earth into sky. But that is not the sign of divine might. It is the *Prema*, the *sadhana* that is effective, universal and ever present. That is the unique sign.

I have come to light the lamp of love in your hearts, to see that it shines day by day with added lustre.

A bubble of water is born out of water. It is made up of water. It ultimately mixes with water and disappears. As in this analogy, man is like a bubble and *Narayan* is like the source of water. Man is born out of *Narayan,* is made up of Him and ultimately merges with Him. What else can I tell you? This is the simple and elemental truth.

A clean, uncontaminated mind is like a fully blossomed, fragrant rose. It refreshes and pleases. It can rise and reach the foot stool of God in heaven.

A discontented man is as good as lost. A man without love is as good as dead.

A healthy body is the best container for a healthy mind; a healthy heart is the temple of God.

A life of *sadhana* involves the dedication of all acts to God, the offering of whatever one does or thinks or speaks at the feet of God.

A moment of concentrated prayer from the heart is enough to melt and move God; hours of shouting do not count.

A person who does not render service is not a human being. He is worse than a beast. We should never give up service—service is our breath. Service is our life. Service is our goal.

At all times, engage yourself in serving others. There is no greater *sadhana* than this.

Be convinced that the service to men is the only means by which you can serve God. Be convinced that men are all living cells in the body of God. Be fair, be true, be strong in your convictions. Then you have My blessings in all that you undertake.

Act as you speak. Speak as you feel. Do not play false to your own conscience by forcibly enslaving it and embarking on actions not approved by it.

Be good, do good, see good, this is the way that leads to God.

Believe that there is no morality higher than truth, there is no prayer more fruitful than Seva.

Bhajan cleanses and purifies the atmosphere by its vital vibrations. It inspires, instructs, it calls and comforts.

Bhakti is as essential for experiencing atomic bliss as blood is essential for the body.

Bhakti must be totally selfless, natural and heartfelt.

Be wherever you like. Do whatever you choose. Remember this well that what you do is known to Me. I am the inner ruler of all.

Be simple and sincere.

Bliss is the experience when the soul is known, anguish if the truth remains unknown. The knower of God verily becomes Him.

Bring Me all the evil in you and leave it there. Then take from Me what I have... love.

Bring Me the depths of your mind, no matter how grotesque, how cruel, ravaged by doubts or disappointments, I know how to treat them. I will not reject you. I am your mother.

Bring to Me your sorrows and griefs, worries and anxieties and take from Me joy and peace, courage and confidence.

Bring your heart to Me and win by heart. Bring your promise to me and I shall give you My promise but first see that your promise is genuine and sincere. See that your heart is pure.

By chanting the name of the Lord sanctify your time. By singing His glory, sanctify your life. Always continuously strive to develop a pure heart for the welfare of the world.

Calamity, danger and death cannot be avoided for all time. They are inevitable factors of life and you have to learn to live bravely with them.

Can we say 'This is good' and 'That is bad', when both this and that are God's creations?

Cleanse your emotions, passions, impulses, attitudes, reactions. This is the essence of spiritual discipline.

Command the mind, regulate your conduct, keep your heart straight and clear, then you will get the grace of God.

Come to Me with empty hands; I shall fill your hands with gifts and grace. Come just one step forward, I shall take a hundred towards you.

Constant dwelling with the name of the Lord gives that unshakeable peace which is unaffected by the ups and downs of life.

Contentment is the most precious treasure. Contentment alone can lead man to the goal of life, the attainment of divinity.

Control of speech is the best ornament and armament.

Continue your worship of your chosen God along the lines already familiar to you and you will find that you are coming nearer and nearer to Me. For all names and all forms are Mine. Call Me by any name—Krishna, Allah or Christ.

Cultivate a nearness with Me in the heart and it will be rewarded. Then you too will acquire some fraction of that Supreme Love. Be confident that you will all be liberated. Let Me assure you that this *dharma swarup*, this divine body, has not come in vain. It will succeed in averting the crisis that has come upon humanity.

Desire is a storm, greed is a whirlpool, pride is precipice, attachment is an avalanche and ego is a volcano. Discard these and you will be liberated.

Dedicate all your thoughts and aspirations to God and surrender yourself to the will of the Divine.

Desire leads to despair.

Desire plus life is man; Life minus desire is God.

Deeds result in joy or grief, prosperity or poverty, gain or loss, pleasure or pain. Deeds direct and decide our destiny for us.

Develop the quality of love and always seek the welfare of mankind.

Develop *Sathya* and *Prema* and then you need not even pray to Me to grant you this and that. Everything shall be added into you, unasked.

Devotion is a complete surrender: It is not a part-time affair or something taken on credit.

Devotion to duty is the highest form of worship to God.

Devotion truly means worshipping the Lord, not caring for the fruits of one's actions.

Do all *karma* as actors in a play; keeping your identity separated and not attaching yourself too much to your role.

Do you know how much I feel when I find that, in spite of My arrival *bodha* and *upadesha*. You have not yet started *sadhana.* You simply praise Me and strew compliments such as I am the treasure house of grace, the ocean of *ananda*, etc. Take up the name and dwell upon its sweetness, imbibe it and roll it on your tongue, taste its essence, contemplate on its magnificence, and make a part of yourself and grow strong in spiritual life. That is what pleases Me.

Do your work well as Puja—an offering at the Lord's feet—and you will be amply rewarded with joy, peace, restfulness and rapture. Work is worship. Duty is God.

Do not seek to measure Me or evaluate Me: I am beyond your understanding.

Do not try to find fault with others, search, rather, for your own.

Do not talk too much.

Duty without love is deplorable, duty with love is desirable. Love without duty is divine.

Dwell always in the thought of God; remind yourself of the glory and majesty of God: That is enough religious discipline for you.

Duty is God, work is worship, I say again. Even the tiniest work is a flower placed at the feet of God.

Ego lives by getting and forgetting. Love lives by giving and forgiving.

Eight types of flowers can be offered to God: (a) Non-violence, (b) Control of the senses, (c) Compassion towards all beings, (d) Truth, (e) Meditation, (f) Peace, (g) Humility, (h) Devotion.

The end of wisdom is freedom, the end of education is character, the end of culture is perfection, and the end of knowledge is love.

The essence of all religious teachings is that you should deep your heart clean.

Essentially, there is only one religion, the religion of humanity.

Every sorrow is a test for God, every failure is a stepping stone.

Expansion is love, contraction is death, experience is truth, seeing is believing.

Extend your hand only for grace from God, ask grace as of right, ask as the child asks the father.

Face the six foes; these are lust, anger, attachment, pride, hatred and greed.

Faith in God is the best reinforcement for spiritual victory. When you travel in the contemplation of God, nothing material can attract you, all else will seem inferior, the company of the godly and humble alone will be relished.

Feel that you are a hundred per cent dependent on God, He will look after you and save you from harm and injury.

Fill your heart with love for everyone. Have firm faith that each one indeed is a brother or a sister to you. In talk and conversation never use harsh words. If you speak harshly, you are hurting the feelings of the other person. Always remember that whoever's feelings you are hurting, you are hurting the feelings of Sai Himself.

Fill your minds with sublime thoughts, and your hearts with divine feelings.

For a person who is full of love, the powers of *Maya* cannot do any harm. *Maya* can only cause problems to those who do not have love in them.

For all happiness and good luck, your actions in your previous life are responsible, your attempts during this life are not the cause.

God examines the purity of our hearts, God wants our love to be free and full.

God is Love. Live in Love.

God is the nearest, the dearest, the most loving, the most eager Companion, Comrade and Kinsman for man.

God is your true Friend. He is with you all the time. He will never leave you at any time at any place. Believe in this that God only is your true Friend and follow Him.

God never fails those who call on Him sincerely and in faith,
God is the source of all love and humility.

God will never disown you, for He is your very core, your basic
reality.

God's grace can destroy the effects of past *karma* or modify its
rigour. If the laws of *karma* are unbreakable, why do sages and
scripture recommend spiritual discipline, living a good life and
cultivation of virtue? *Prarabdha* (the effects of past *karma*)
will melt like mist before the sun if you win the grace of God.
God's love is more intense than the love of a thousand mothers,
it is not offered to satisfy any desire.

**Grief and joy are inseparable companions. Grief or joy:
Welcome them as God's grace.**

Hands that help are holier than lips that pray.

Happiness is only an interval between two miseries; it is the
gap between moments of happiness.

Have faith that Swami is with you at all places, at all times.

He who dedicates his time, skill and strength to service, can
never meet defeat, distress or disappointment. He will have no
foe, no fatigue, no fear.

He who is able to fully control his senses can attain liberation
or *moksha*.

However you are, you are Mine, I will never give you up.
Wherever you are, you are near Me. You cannot go beyond My
reach.

The human heart is an ocean whose depth none can gauge nor
can anyone limit its horizon.

I am always with you, behind you, beside you, in front of you,
in your very heart.

I am an example and inspiration, whatever I do or omit to do;
My life is a commentary on My message.

I am aware of your innermost thoughts and deepest desires.

I am aware of the past, present and future of every one of you,
I know why you suffer and how you can escape sufferings.

I am beyond the reach of the most intensive enquiry and the
most meticulous measurement.

I am ever new and ever ancient. I am never born, nor do I die.

I am in every one of you and so I become aware of your
slightest wave of thought.

I am in your hearts, you are in Mine. Do not be misled into
doubt and distress.

I am infinite, I am immeasurable, I am unique, I am incomparable. Equal to Myself, I am My own measure, witness and authority.

I am the Creator, Preserver and Destroyer, nothing will harm him who turns his attention towards Me.

I am the *'Satashya Sathyam'*, the Truth of truths. Why has truth come on earth in human form? To plant in the heart of man the yearning for truth, to place man on the road to truth, to help man to reach truth, by loving instruction and by the final gift of illumination.

I am the embodiment of love and that love is My instrument; Mine is love that is pure, free, selfless and unconditional.

I cannot but tell you one fact; ninety-nine out of a hundred of you do not strive to know My reality. You cannot understand My reality, either today or even after thousands of years of austerity of inquiry, even if all mankind were to join in that effort.

I draw you to Me and then reform and re-shape you.

I give you what you want so that you may want what I want to give you.

I have come to restore love among mankind, to cleanse it of its narrowness and restrictive attitudes. I shall not rest until I reform you all.

I know your name, your degrees, your profession, your status and your history. I know your past, present and future. But you do not know me. That is why sometimes in order to reveal who I am, I myself show my visiting card, something you call a miracle.

I know the agitation of your heart, the inspiration, the waves, the whirlpools, I react to the pain you undergo, the joy that you feel.

I live in the experience that I am one with everyone. I am with everything, every human being. My love flows out to all and I see everyone as Myself. If a person reciprocates My love from the depth of his heart, My love and his love meet in unison and he is cured and transformed.

I long to reside in your hearts, fragrant with the incense of fine virtues, merciful intentions, and compassionate emotions.

I repair broken hearts and fragile minds, warped intellects, feeble resolutions and fading faith.

I shall look after all those who renounce the ego and take refuge in Me.

I shall never give up those who attach themselves to Me, I shall guard you like the lids guard the eyes.

If I had come amongst you as *Narayana* with four arms holding the conch, the wheel, the mace and the lotus, you would have kept Me in a museum and charged a fee for those who seek *darshan*. If I had come as a mere man you would not have respected My teachings and followed them for your own good. So I have to be in this human form with super-human wisdom and powers.

It is enough that you call Me from wherever you are, in My case there is no need for you to travel long distances and spend hard earned money. I shall fulfil all your wishes at your own place.

Karma cleanses the mind if it is done as a dedicatory act, the consequences being left to the will of the Lord.

Know yourself first, all else next.

Let Me tell you this, Mine is no mesmerism, miracle or magic. Mine is genuine divine power.

Life is a journey from 'I' to 'We'.

Life is a search, explore it. Life is a challenge, meet it. Life is a game, play it. Life is a dream, realise it.

Life is a short play on the stage, life is love.

Life is a pilgrimage to God, the holy spot is there, the road lies before you. Start with courage, faith, joy and steadiness; You are bound to succeed.

Life is the best teacher.

Like a mother, I will be tender and soft and give you happiness. Like a father, I shall punish you and criticise you, when needed.

The Lord's name is sweeter than nectar. Let the Lord's sweet Name dance on your tongue.

Love all, serve all.

Love fosters peace, peace nourishes truth, truth confers bliss and bliss is God.

Love God with all your heart, with all your soul, with all your mind and with all your strength.

Love in thought is Truth. Love in action is right conduct. Love in understanding is peace. Love in feeling is non-violence.

Love is My form, truth is My breath, peace is My food. My life is My message.

Love is divine; the love of God means love of humility.

Love is the essence of worship, love is one big instrument for the constant remembrance of God.

Love the Lord's creation as much as the Lord Himself. Then the tree of life will yield the sweet fruit of *madhur bhakti.*

Make full use of the skill, capacity, courage and confidence that you are endowed with, then God will bless you.

Make your house a small *mandir,* meditate in your shrine room, sing *bhajans* with your children.

Man is born to share and serve, not to grab and grieve.

Man's foremost duty is to make the stream of divine love flow throughout the world.

Many words harm the mind. Few words charm the soul.

Measure the height you have reached with the yardstick of virtue, serenity, fortitude and equanimity.

My affection and love for each one of you is that of thousand mothers. Do not deny yourself that affection, that love, by denying Me your love.

Miracles are the spontaneous and natural expression of *avatarhood*.

My mission is to grant you courage and joy, to drive away weakness and fear.

My task is not merely to cure and console and remove individual misery. But it is something far more important.

My task is to open your eyes to the glory of the *Vedas* and to convince you that the Vedic injunctions, when put into practice, will yield the promised results. My *prema* towards the *Vedas* is only matched by my *prema* towards humanity.

No one can escape the consequences of one's action, whether good or bad. Whatever one does, he cannot escape from its reaction.

No one can understand my mystery. The best you can do is to get immersed in it. The mysterious, indescribable power has come within the reach of all.

Of the twenty-four hours of the day, use six for earning and spending, six for contemplating on God, six for sleep and six for service to others.

Purify your hearts, your thoughts, feelings, emotions, speech, strengthen your nobler impulses. Then no panic can unnerve you. Nothing can shake your stability.

Only those who have recognised My love and experienced that love, can assert that they glimpsed My reality. For the path of love is the royal road that leads mankind to me.

Peace is the most priceless possession of man. It is the sign of virtue, character, a willingness to serve, a readiness to renounce, a calm spirit of resignation, an awareness of the evanescence of material wealth, of the cool agitationless lake of joy in the heart.

Pleasure is an interval between two pains.

Prayer alone makes life happy, harmonious and worth living in this universe. Prayer brings man and God together and with every sigh, nearer and nearer.

Prayer is the yearning one experiences to awaken the divinity latent in the heart. Prayer is not pronouncing of words.

Praying is your task. What happens to the prayer, is dependent on the grace of God.

Purify your vision. Sweeten your speech. Sanctify your deeds—that way lies liberation.

The real renunciation that one has to make is the giving up of the evil qualities of *kama* (desire), *krodha* (anger) and *lobha* (greed).

Realise the brotherhood of man and the fatherhood of God by your selfless service and *prema*. Serve all and try to realise the unity in all.

The relief and joy that you give to the sick and the sad, reach Me. For, I am in their hearts and I am the one they call out for.

Rely in the Lord and accept whatever is your lot. He knows what to give and when.

Remember Me always. Believe in me heart and soul and then you will be most benefited.

Remember that your mother and father are the first people whom you should regard as God.

Sai is beyond the keenest intellect, the sharpest brain. So do not try to delve into Me. Develop faith and *shraddha* and derive *ananda* through prema. This is the utmost you can do. Do that and benefit.

Sai is ever-willing and ever-ready to help and assist at all times and at all places. It is this that gives you to Sai.

Sai is Infinite Love. It is this love that pervades and appears in the entire universe around us. This love is seated ever in your hearts. So you are not different from the universe. The universe is Sai, you are Sathya Sai.

See good, do good, be good. This is the way to God.

Seek work, worship and wisdom. Avoid wealth, wine and women.

Service is worship. Each act of service is a flower placed at the feet of God.

Start the day with love, spend the day with love, fill the day with love, end the day with love. That is the way to God.

Steadiness, faith and love are the essential requisites for earning the grace of God.

Strive—that is your duty, Yearn—that is your task, Struggle—that is your assignment. If only you do these sincerely and steadily, God cannot keep back for long the reward of realisation.

Take as much bliss as you can from Me and leave Me with all your sorrows.

Shed just one tear, I shall wipe a hundred from your eyes.

The correct discipline to acquire the *nishkaama* attitude is dedication, and dedication is possible only when you have intense faith in God. That faith becomes steady through *sadhana*.

The acts of Sai are always selfless, sacred and beneficial. Sai has never caused harm to anyone. He is establishing the path of truth, the holy path to God-realisation. Love is My highest miracle.

The Sai name will arouse ecstatic delight filling the entire world, every inch of it. This is the human form in which the divine entity, every facet of the divine principle, that is to say, all the names and forms ascribed by man to God, are manifest.

True devotion is that which enables your love to flow constantly towards God, regardless of any results, without expecting any regard.

True love consists in serving the Lord, recognising the Lord in every one and serving everyone in the same way.

Unless God's grace and human effort come together, the result cannot be achieved.

Visualise God, seek God, merge in God—that is the duty of man.

Watch your words, watch your actions, watch your thoughts, watch you character, watch your heart.

When the ego goes, the Light of God flows.

Whatever you do, wherever you are, remember that I am with you, in you and will save you from conceit and error.

Why fear when I am here? Pull all your faith in Me. I shall guide and guard you.

Wherever My glory is sung, I bestow My divine presence. Whoever among the devotees dedicates all acts to Me with no other thoughts, whoever meditates on Me, serves Me, worships Me, remembers Me, knows that I am always with him, ever providing for him. I bear all his burdens and guarantee him fulfilment of his needs and security.

Yearning leads to surrender and surrender gives the highest joy. Leave everything to God's will, accept whatever happens, whether pleasant or painful.

Yesterday has deceived you and gone. Tomorrow is a doubtful visitor. Today is a good friend. Hold fast to it.

You think of Me, I am with you. You need not come where I am.

Your heart is My home.

Your heart must be transparent like glass with spiritual light within illuminating the whole world.

Your welfare, your happiness, your progress and your noble qualities; these alone will please Sai and fill him with happiness.

Appendix II

THE FIGURE THAT AN *AVATAR* MAKES: SOME IMAGES OF THE DIVINE MADE HUMAN

There comes a phase in human history which may be called both crucial and climactic and is also full of rich and immense possibilities. It is a time when only through time is *time* conquered. We are indeed living in such a calamitous and auspicious moment of history. The world stands perilously poised at the brink of a precipice ready to be blown over and broken into innumerable fragments, almost to be wiped out of existence. In this ego of anxiety when the black pall and ominous hover, annihilation and destruction threaten the very existence of mankind and triumphant march of evil seems to bring the doomsday or *pralaya* closer to us, the saints and the sages take recourse to prayer in the hope that some miracle would take place and the inevitable catastrophe, the cosmic dance of death, would somehow be averted and the superior grace of the Saviour would descend to make possible the complete spiritual redemption and regeneration of mankind. The concept of the divine descent on earth or incarnation is central to Indian thought and philosophy. Amongst the Hindu trinity, Brahma the creator, Vishnu, the preserver and Shiva, the destroyer, it is Vishnu who incarnates himself in human form from time to time to remind man of his essential divinity and help him achieve his destiny, which is a merging with the infinite.

It is indeed unique and exciting to think that at a certain point of human history, when the decline of religion is total

and the ceremony of innocence is drowned and the good seem
to lack all conviction and the worst is full of passionate
intensity, the coming of the Lord is anticipated. Even in the
Bible, there is an explicit reference to the Second Coming and
Lord Krishna in his Song Celestial has made the declaration
that, whenever the eclipse of *dharma* is certain and most
perceptible, he incarnates himself from age to age. Thus, the
advent of the Lord on earth has been made actual. In Thretha
it was Lord Rama who appeared in Ayodhya to destroy the
demons and kill Ravana, who symbolised the evil and restore
dharma on a firm footing. Again in *Dwapar*, Krishna
descended on the soil of Mathura and Gokul to destroy a whole
galaxy of demons and living embodiments of sin and evil and
helped the virtuous *Pandavas* achieve the final victory over
the *Kauravas* in the battle of Kurukshetra. And, what is more
important is that he enunciated the doctrine of *karma* for the
benefit of humanity, a gospel that presented the quintessence
of the *Vedas* and the *Upanishads* and all Indian scriptures,
something to live by. In spite of their supreme might and
divine powers, both Rama and Krishna lived on the human
plane and offered comfort and solace to all who had the good
fortune of coming into contact with them. It is indeed
incredible to think of the singular good fortune of all those
noble and beautiful souls, even of the demons and evil-doers
who met their doom at the hands of the Lord. They must have
been immortal people who, on account of noble and virtuous
deeds in their past lives, had earned the unique distinction of
knowing the Lord at first hand and been the recipients of his
love and grace. We can only contemplate and marvel at the
singular and salutary good fortune of the virtuous souls,
certain claimants, to entry into the kingdom of heaven.

But, once again, history seems to have repeated itself, for,
at the present juncture of history, in the age called *Kaliyuga*
humanity has been blessed with the singular good fortune of
being contemporaneous with the Lord, who had incarnated
Himself in human form at Puttaparthi in Andhra Pradesh. As
Sri Sathya Sai Baba has, time and again, disclosed the reality
of his divine incarnation we have to believe in him and try to
get at the mystery of his divinity through continuous *sadhana*,
ardour and love and, of course, through our own perceptions,

and experiences. Sri Sathya Sai Baba has disclosed that Lord Shiva, pleased by the devotion and continual penance of sage Bharadwaj, appeared before him as he lay frozen and paralysed on the vast sheets of ice in the Himalayas and assured him that he would appear in his lineage and *gotra* in *Kaliyuga* in a cycle of triple Sai *avatars*. He would first appear as Sai Baba at Shirdi, Maharashtra, representing the full powers of Lord Shiva. He further declared that eight years after attaining his *maha samadhi* at *Shirdi*, he would appear again at Puttaparthi in Andhra Pradesh and enact the full cycle of his *avatar* as Shiva and Shakti rolled into one. Sri Sathya Sai Baba, on his part has made the declaration that he would appear as Prema Sai in Gunaparthi in the Mandya district of Karnataka after taking his *maha samadhi* at the age of ninety-five. He has also stated that Prema Sai would walk incognito on earth for several years before declaring his real identity and *avataric* mission.

Thus, through the instrumentality of all these incarnations, the declared mission of the *avatar* would be fully achieved and humanity would be utterly transformed and the reign of truth, love, peace and non-violence would reign supreme on earth, justifying the poet's saying:

The Earth's great age begins a new
The golden years return.

Be that as it may, it is nice to imagine that we are contemporaneous with the Lord of the universe and can travel down south to stand face to face with the luminous and blazing sun and crave for His redemptive grace.

While it is difficult to define and explicate precisely the figure that an *avatar* makes since we are too close to the times, we can form our own impressions mainly through our immediate perceptions and personal experiences.

ISBN 81-207-1564-0

STERLING PAPERBACKS
An imprint of
STERLING PUBLISHERS PVT. LTD.

9 788120 715646

Rs. 85